Of The Path And Of The Drops

Shahab Shamloo (Silent)

AuthorHouse™ UK Ltd.
500 Avebury Boulevard
Central Milton Keynes, MK9 2BE
www.authorhouse.co.uk
Phone: 08001974150

First published by AuthorHouse   3/5/2011

ISBN: 978-1-4567-7609-1 (sc)

Of the Path	Originally in English
Intercross	Originally in English
Plunder	Originally in English
Again my Iran….Ah	Translation
Three Songs for Wild , tamed ….	Translation
Infected Inheritance	Translation
The Breeze of Freedom	Translation
The Troubled Waters	Translation
Satan and Ashes	Translation
I will not Return	Translation
Rain of Brains	Translation
Creation	Translation
Ransack	Translation
Home Enchained	Originally in English
Whispers of Chains	Translation
Reflection	Originally in English
Elections	Originally in English
Memory	Translation
Slaughtered Sacrifice	Translation
Ah and Thirst ….my Country	Translation
Of the Drops	Translation
Beat	Translation
Happy New Year	Originally in English
More Lovingly	Translation
The Arising	Translation
Lovingly	Translation
Fate	Translation
Upon the lips of every Stranger	Translation
Golden Thoughts	Translation
Sunk	Translation
Conquered	Translation
For the Mourning of our Nation	Translation
Conundrum	Translation
Load	Originally in English
Temptation	Translation
Heavenly Caress	Translation
In Mourning	Translation
Beamish	Translation
The Sheikh of Palm Trees and Oasis	Translation

In the Name of Humanity

In these lost times in which human beings fear their reflection and flee from their own homes , in this colorful city that is all so vibrant with life and lust resting upon the borderlines of two continents in which cold faces stare upon you like a mobile dollar bill , I thought , now that I have no intentions of returning to my motherland for the sake of protecting my life , I would prepare my poetry collection for publishing .

And as I had plenty of time awaiting for the reputed smuggler who as a result of good fortune speaks the same language with the sweet Dari accent to ship us with an anonymous Bill of Lading to a North European country , where it is said that they respect the freedom and dignity of a human being and have engraved his rights within a solid non-deteriorating stone in the clearest and most readable manner possible , I also made the English translations of my works . As a result of being raised in a bilingual home I had been thought to think in two languages from the start of my childhood enabling my words to take shape at times in Persian and at times in English depending on the necessity or the substance of the relative descending inspiration , therefore the translations have not come out that bad and I am personally satisfied with the work up to 50-60% .

Also in order to enrich the English text I have at times increased or reduced from the authentic material while preserving the core essence , even at times making some poetic changes and adjustments to enhance and evolve the meaning and to induce some basic added value .

There are some poems included within this book that were originally written in English which I have not translated into Persian as I sensed that this would not contribute to the significance of the finished work , with the exception of one poem titled :
"Of The Path" .

I should also indicate that in my opinion not all of my works are of significant artistic value , and I only praise poetry which flows out without the slightest contemplation within the artist's absence of consciousness , where his words take form in some distant dry blazing fields with the burning fists of it's flames flickering towards the

heavens in destructive protest , or by a tranquil oasis spring where the deer of innocence gather to revive their body and spirit seeking refuge from fierce merciless predators , or in the dark depths of some unexplored jungle with juicy exotic fruits yet to be tasted by man , and or upon the thrashing stormy waves of some lost savage sea attempting to infringe the known shores of mortal imagination .
Like the poems that came into existence during my solitary confinement in Evin prison , inscribed into my soul with the blood of my heart with no pen nor paper which I would whisper to myself to provide a glimmer of companionship in my lightless nights of utter isolation and hopelessness .

Although I must honestly admit that in some of these works initially only a few verses had flowed out to later be completed in distinct and thorough reflection , but many of these poems have been written in the above described state of restless unconsciousness without the slightest adjustments and are being presented in their raw form .
This is why I have eliminate many poems from this book , so that most of the works could be the product of this mesmerizing entity .
Therefore I assume it will better to call this book a selection rather than a collection .

I also believe that a writer or poet must study and review the works of others if not a 1000 times more at least a 100 times more than what he actually writes , in order to create a strong foundation for the waters of his inspiration to flow upon and for his words to find a solid structure and render a penetrating effect .

And I truly wish that all people would read and study at least a few times more than what they think or even more importantly a few times more than the actions they carry out ;
Especially us Iranians ! .
For if we had acquired knowledge of the destructive force of political Islam and how the verses in the Koran which strictly preached love , kindness , and compassion initially written in Mecca were all transformed to teachings of bloodshed and intolerance immediately after the Islamic army conquered Medina and established the first Islamic regime by the way of the sword .

And we would have known that any change that is induced through violent means shall have to be sustained through the same aggressive methods .
And we would have known that democracy can not be achieved through religion as it advocates prejudice within it's own existence , and not through any belief that comes into power , other than the belief of human rights , and freedom for all .
And we would have known better not to commit this mass social suicide we called an Islamic revolution !
But I do not know if it's due to arrogance or laziness that we prefer others to do the hard work of studying for us and then brief us on the highlights of their contemplation .
As a result of this they inject whatever serves their purpose best into our minds .
And we nod our heads in confirmation with our inflated lips and emotionless mongoloid faces , later swearing on the life of our children , hands on heart , that what we've heard is the absolute truth !

Anyhow let's get back to my tale , for this tale will not reach a conclusion within a few pages , and at the moment we will not find the earth to implant this seed of pain .

Now in this time and age that is all so deranged in which the noble peace prize is awarded to a person who has the potential to launch massive military attacks and who conducts contracts for the sales of high tech. arms and state of the art arsenal in order to return petrodollars into his pockets on a regular basis , and to pay off the salary of the workers of his arms factories with the blood of people like me , in these alien times in which they loan off God in skyrocketing interests rates in the Euro currency , in these times where death is gift wrapped and forwarded via post , in these lost times in which animal-faced leaders fabricate suicidal bombs from the desperation , poverty , and dire hardships of others , and in these times in which nothing rhymes where in our beloved country the most mind-quaking atrocities are being carried out in the name of the Lord , by the blood trickling iron claws of Mullah-Military rulers who claim to be the representatives of God upon earth and who call themselves the chosen ones .

That one is dressed in a suit of the finest Italian wool with ironed lines on his trouser so neatly sharp that they could virtually split a melon who with one gesture of his hand thousands fall to the swelling earth in blood , and this one resembles a caveman from the stone-ages who kills in the classical fashion with a hatchet and a butcher's trunk one by one in turn .

Both claim to be acting in favor of your rights !

Yes people , in these strange times the desperate dog has every right to lose the way to it's master's home .

I have always thought about this now I will say it :

What is the value or to say more precisely what kind of a positive effect can poetry and art in general have in such mind-hazing times ?

Can it generate prospering alteration and or invite human-beings back to their humanistic roots ?

I know this : If poetry or any other work of art for any reason does not have the capacity to provoke sudden comprehensive change , it should at least have the capability to captivate the reader to such an extent as to withdraw him from his current atmosphere in exploration , and when returning him to his realistic world have added minimum 1 cm to his height and to his values , opening his mind and empowering him with the courage to think , feel , and speak more freely . If not well than sadly it can only be considered as a snack for the mind , or a snickers bar for the fat man's heart , nothing more nothing less .

In any case until a work of art is not shared publically with others and does not gain recognition and enkindle criticism , the artist can in no way accomplish any kind of improvement .

And we the people of my beloved nation are just at the start of the long and winding road leading to democracy , and we are just learning that democracy requires a democratic mind , and we are just learning to hear all voices and to respect all the beliefs of others ,

And we are just learning that sustainable freedom can not be achieved by the way of the gun , and we are just learning that having solely one color in our society is meaningless and worthless , even if that color is green , and we are just learning that colors need harmony and contrast to thrive and shine , and we are just learning not to impose our beliefs and thoughts upon others no matter how flawless and functional we perceive them to be , and we are just learning not to insult the opinions

of others no matter how imperfect and irrational we assume them to be , and we are just learning .....
Maybe one of these days we will learn !

If I have in any way affronted the pearl-like convictions of anyone anywhere in this book , I sincerely apologize in advance . It was truly out of my hands and my heart was filthy aching .

Before I forget let me also mention that since the past year I have commenced to work on my first fictional novel , which is based on the true story of my life but has been enhanced with the explicit use of fictional characters and provocative imagination .
The story has been circulating around my heart and brain for more than 10 years now and I have just finished around 100 pages in the most dispersed fashion conceivable that can only be attributed to an unstable character with continuously fluctuating emotions and perceptions .
It would be illogical to impose any kind of deadline upon myself for completing this novel as I want it to come out perfect , but I hope to finalize it within a few years .

So here you are : "Of the Path and Of the Drops"

I am always open to any kind of suggestions and I welcome all criticism no matter how dark or brutal they may be .

So friends please do not be stingy : shahabshamloo@yahoo.com

"Of the Path"

Dedicated to Harout Khatchadourian

My eyes ;
Two diamond stars ,
Stolen from King Solomon's treasure ,
To shine in the eclipse of Crucifixion ,
And to witness the fall of Jerusalem .

The filth-oozing crust of my burning skin :
The reptile ripples of the Arabian desert .

My tongue ,
Is the path upon the silk road ,
That leads from the palace court of Haroon Rashid ,
To the dungeons of Evin prison . *

And my hands ;
Two shaking olive leaves ,
Feeding from my veins that beat ,
With the heart of the Euphrates .

October-2010-S.Shamloo

*Evin Prison : Notorious political prison in Tehran

"Intercross"

You are ,
Breathing poetry in motion .
A living never-ending novel ,
Who's destiny is determined ,
At the right or left hand turn ,
Of the intercross section .

October-2010 –Tehran
S.Shamloo

"Plunder"

And we watched ,
With clouded eyes ,
The auctioning of our lands .
The pipelines continued to pump ,
And Mohammad continued to hump ,
And the prisoners clapped with severed hands …

Summer 2009 Tehran

"Again my Iran : Ah"

Again my Iran : Ah
Why are you crying from all the grains of your existence ,
From your Alborz* standing high , down to your ports of sad glory ,
With so much piercing persistence ?

Enough ; you have taken me ,
Driven me out of myself with your wild cries of pain
Upon your infertile soil wipe off the blood and tears of your resistance
.

With enchained hands and my imploded heart ,
you how am I to rebuild ,
Placing my green vision of vast free fields
before you with pleading insistence ?

With this throat thorn torn how am I to cry out for assistance ,
with this body ruptured to the bone ,
how am I to lay my head upon the earth ,
To hear from where your riding warrior is coming ,
How far and from which distance ?

This life is not worth a petty cent ,
without freedom it's not worth being spent ,
Look at my feeble structure ,
it's no longer shaking from the blade of these beastly slayers ,
this I'll sacrifice again and again for your survival in consistence .

I have come from Binalood* to your White River* ,
I have come from black jungles to your rusty mountains ,
I have come from Samarkand to Damavand ,
I have come with my soul's every strand ,
to place my face upon your lovely side in deliverance .

Your earth's every corner , your every epic border ,
tells a tale ; a historic order ,
From the Kurds I've been taught not to weep upon death ,
and from your Wandering wounded Balochis*

I've learned rock desert patience .

The ones you deserted ,
the evil hand of which demonic minded child all so perverted ,
Has replaced your colorful crown
with the magic curse of Allah Akbar in subsistence ?

Where are these people from ,
from which tribe or nation did they come ,
That they implant the seeds of hate deep within your land's fate ,
Are they the bastards of Genghis Khan or Alexander in substance ?

They beheaded your trees ,
set aflame your domes of culture and science ,
Destroyed your houses of wine , feasted on bread from mills
revolving in the blood of your youth all so divine ,
all in the name of Allah ; the host's of Allah's shrine ,
The army of those lizard eating desert nomads in disgusting defiance .

O my lost nation , within your history's pages you'll not find ,
such rulers who plunder upon their own country and kind ,
losing a portion of your precious soil
each night drunken in a humiliating gamble blind ,
damn your star of wicked aberrance !

Summer 2009 Tehran

*Alborz : A mountain range in north central Iran
*Binalood : A mountain range in north western Iran
*White Water : The name of one of Iran's largest rivers in the north of
this country .

*Baluchis : Members of a group of tribes speaking the Baluchi language and inhabiting the province of Balochistan in Pakistan and neighboring areas of Iran, and Afghanistan .

"Three Songs for tamed , wild and moderate animals"

Dedicated to Shakaib and Sha
For all of their kindness

Softening your food with your piss ,
You animal ,
Rolling around in your shit , like this ,
Speaks of your knowledge .
Your master is coming ,
With his club kiss ,
You animal ,

Shut lock your snout ,
And rest , in your blind world bliss .

-

Give me chow ,
Or I'll chew your balls like dogs ,
I have lost all my patience :
Damn it ; it's your fields I plow !

With your intestines ,
The height of my boy ,
I'll measure and determine ,
If not given
My share at the table .
My mold shred bread-cloth
Is not a fable .

-

How long ,
Will you continue to thrash ,
The mass ,
Of my bruised hide ;
Cracked crust slashed ?

Beware !
For this gold convey donkey ,
Thorn thrust trashed
Also has a God .

Hear ,
And seek shelter ,
In fear ;

The weary bray braying ,
Of this wounded beast ,
Has shook the foundations ,
Of your mansions .

One day ,
I'll see you ,
Up to the neck in the swamp ,

Of my shit wastes ,
With your pleading face ,
And your nozzle ,
Quivering with apologetic disgrace .

Summer 2007 Karaj

Your movement and motion ,
Have inspired my contemplation ,
And I hereby summarize ,
All of the force of your biceps and hands ,
All of your screams ,

All of your God's strict commands ,
All of this obscure earthly mess ,
Within a tender kiss and caress .
Baghdad , gone
Bengal , gone
Bread , gone
Bellies , fat full fed , gone
Until we washed our rotten sacredness ,
In the troubled water of the Ganges ,
Warp and weft .
By the temples ,
Who's torches were set alight ,
By the hands of our forefather's ,
Two thousand years ago ,

And the troubled waters ,
Mourn in flames ,
Eternally .

Autumn 2006 Tehran

"Satan and Ashes"

Satan and ashes ,
Mouth to mouth ,
Mind to mind .

The mind ,
United with the devil ,
And the heart ,
With God .

Thoughts ,
Entrapped , in freedom's cage ,
And the mouth ,
In rambling curse , enraged .

Ashes and Satan ,
From Kabul ,
To Baghdad ,
And from Baghdad ,
To Pasargad . *

Summer-2007-Tehran

*Pasargadae (Persian: پاسارگاد), the capital of Cyrus the Great (559-530 BC)
and also his last resting place, was a city in ancient Persia,

"I will not return"

Once more ,
Again from within ,
Time after rhyme ,
In pause ,
I have spit out ,
My thick saliva ,
Like an infectious curse ,
Towards your city ,
So hustling ,
So hollow ,
And again ,
Inevitably condemned ,
I have returned to it's dense acetous air ,
That like high rusty iron walls ,
Protect all that is nothing from within .

Oh you God of sorrow ,
What is the cause and purpose ,
Of this obscure creation ,
So unhallowed   ?

****

Oh you ,
Who become aroused ,
Up to your rims ,
With the saturated scent ,
Of your ladies' panties ;
I will not return towards you .

Oh you ,
Who with your piercing sticks ,
Auction off your mothers ,

Around the sweltering mind-spinning square of summer ,
I will not return towards you .

Oh you ,
Who dig graves ,
For your elders in advance ,
I will not return towards you .

Summer 2007 Tehran

"Rain of Brains"

The sound of a crisp thought ,
Circulating around your pillow .

The flight of a fat flourished notion ,
Into the distant impossible horizon .

And a trembling claw of the night ,
That is choking you fatal tight ,
Until ashes rain ,
From the explosion of your brain ,
In the sky's four corners ,
To sit upon the head of the city's mourners .

Winter 2007 Tehran

"Creation"

The boiling of an inspiration ,
And the fluctuation of emotions .

A tear ,
A smile ,
And the trembling of a hand ;
Then you came into creation ….

Winter 2007 Tehran

"Ransack"

O Lord ,
How was I to know ,
That a flower ,
Can within it's own roots ,
Become enchained ,
Twisting tight around it's neck ,
Fatally ingrained .

*****

You don't know ,
The dark sorrow
Of your eyes' sunset ,
In the cloud shadows ,
Of your heart-dripping lashes
My kind-bosom love .

Upon the graves ,
Of your forefathers ,
I witnessed ,
The blossoming of your red tears ,
Vintage ; 1400 years
And then I cried upon myself ,
Like my Caspian sea ,
                    Lovingly .

Autumn 2007 Karaj

"Home Enchained"

The circular fluctuation of your brain ,
Within an impossible vacuum .

Passing through the tight tunnel of hatred
To off-load your burden ,
Upon the immense green fields
You have sought at the price of your soul .

When they crack open your sister's head ,
With a golden club ,
Is your life worth a bite of bread ?

You gaze within a haze of heat
At the chains around your heart ,
That have been nailed in the earth
Of the borderline of your home .
Awaiting the moment of explosion ,
Of that iron-ripping beat ,
To keep the rhythm to the song :
"Living once , Dying once " .

Summer 2009

"Whispers of Chains"

Between being and becoming ,
Space and time ,
Are boundless ....
Drift afloat .

In love ,
Verse and rhyme ,
Have no profoundness ,
Passions do not pass
Through the throat .

This is the whirling echo of the chains' whisper ,
That is shaking the alleys ,
Up to their teeth ....
Can you hear from beneath ? :

"Cry out ,
Cry about ,
You the crazy ,
You possessed ,
You hopeless ,
You oppressed ,
You enchained ,
Within your pain .

Shout out ,
Shout out without a dagger ,
Shout out ,
Without a doubt .

From deep within ,
Loud ,
Shout about .
You aliens from yourselves .

You the angry ,
You hungry ,
With your dignity upon the shelves ,

Sigh out ,
Sigh about ,
Sigh out to the sun ,
Until you stir up a blazing storm ,
Throughout the dancing wild spruces ,
Sigh out until it's done .

******

Now
The space ,
Is the space that is paced ,
By the calling of battle drums
To the piercing cry of a headless warrior .

The time ,
Is the time ,
To hang every ,
Religion selling store owner ,
From all the willows .

Spring 2008 Karaj

"Reflection"

A cry is up-roaring within my soul
It seems ,
From the purest air of the mountains .

A love is sparkling within my eyes
It seems ,
From the earliest springs and fountains .

A flavor is bursting within my mouth
It seems ,
From the most exotic fruits of the deepest jungles .

An inspiration is baking within my mind ,
From the most ancient volcanoes ,
To erupt , fresh , in flames , refined …

I have lost my mother tongue
In the twinkling reflection of the leaves ,
Within this glimpse , this moment ; so undefined ….

Oh lord , Of God , oh Allah
Or whatever they may call you ;
Blah , Blah , Blah ,
Untie my chained hands and ,
Open my clinch fists
So that I may take within my embrace
Your everything and all .
From sky to rain
From the earth to every grain ,
From every river to water fall …..

Summer 2008 Tehran

"Elections"

Congratulations ;
Your monkey man has won again .
God is Great , fuck the people ,
Rigging is not a sin .

Cheat to defeat ,
Oppress to possess ,
Condemnation , execution ,
Now all lay at the stroke of your holy pen .

"Memory"

Current in the earth body ;
Your womb of essence ;

Will you remain ,
Or will you depart ?

Will you end ,
Or will you commence ?

All vision ,
Fades , playing in the vague shadows ,
But you can hear every grain in motion .

A light-like sound ,
Flaming ,
Calls you alluringly ,
With a scream intense ,
And a familiar image ,
Is embedded into your memory ,
From an eternal distance .

Winter 2007 Karaj

"Slaughtered Sacrifice"

Dedicated to Benazir Buto
Who's murder wrenched my heart
And numbed my mind .

Burn to burn ,
Everything and all ,

Burn strong ,
Burn aflame ,
Burn with no embers of shame ….

With the blood yearning knowledge of your prophets ,
All drowning in the fascination of vulgar needs ,
                                        So untamed .

Burn and burn ,
Everything that blooms
Burn all that is to become ,
Burn for and from ,

O , you sleeping beyond the borders of history ,
Close your eyes ,
To the bleeding cry of your children ,
In painful plea .
Rollover and rest sedated ,
In your coffin shrine of hatred .

Burn and burn ,
Burn outside and within ,
Burn again and again .

Burn to burn ,
Turn after turn .
Burn in blinding deceit .

Our beautiful maiden of the east ,
Slaughtered to sacrifice ,

Before your God's feet .

Winter 2007 Tehran

"Ah and thirst….my country"

Ah ,
The dying sun of my dreams ,
Shine , at least ,
A mere moment , to gleam
Upon my nation's frosty body .

What words ,
What book ,
These tears ,
Can interpret ,
Can distinguish .

Which sigh ,
What water ,
Which cry ,
This thirst
Can quench ,
This flame
Can relinquish   ?

Winter 2007 Karaj

"Of the Drops"

A polo ball of crumbling lead ,
And the rhythmic hoofs of black and white horses
Inside your head .

Your eternal internal mobile emptiness ,
Has breached the aviation borders of mars ,

And God and satin ,
A few centuries ago ,
Agreed upon your fate
With a mocking smile ,
Behind closed gates

Ah , this golden Farvahar* ,
Around your neck ,
Seems to have no more effect .
Fashion style your chest hair ,
And hands on wheel ,
Make a rap-star pose ,
Riding free with no care   ;

"Fatima" has said goodbye
To her gardens of floral ,
To find her God ,
In the distant desert lands ,
Look at her hands ,
They are always raised towards the sky ,
Begging the Almighty for two drops to cry .

And "Jela" has sunk into deep contemplation ,
With the pounding of her anticipation ,
That has shredded her veins ,
Waiting for a hand and a friend in frustration ,
To fondle her throbbing overheated virginity .

Ah , silence you little 40 year old boy ,

Who likes to play with his words ,
Like his toys of joy .
Silence you verse drooling fool ,
Now put all of your poems of love and hate ,
Upon a scale and await ,
To see if anyone will grant you ,
A piece of bread ,
At their weight !

You were like a river ,
That formed from the drops of the mountain snow ,
Passed through the valleys , and hills ,
Passed through the rubbish and daily trash and continued to flow ,
Freed yourself of the "Volga" , and united with the "Ganges" ,
To shine and glow ,
What became upon you ,
That you sunk in this endless swamp encircling ,
Of production and consumption ,
Disposal and recycling ?

*****

There is a huge polo game inside your head ,
Silence you little 40 year old boy ,
Silence , you can not raise the blind-deaf dead …

Summer 2009 Tehran

Farvahar :   Symbol of supreme logic in the Zoroastrian faith .
                   Summarized in three main factors :

Good speech , Good deeds , and Good thoughts .

"Beat"

The pounding of your drum heart ,
Has brought down all mirrors in darkness .
For me to trace ,
The humid outlines
Of your blazing face ,
With my fingertips .

Crisis of devices ,
The past of the last ,
Has brought you ,
Into me .

Your nakedness ,
Shakes my entity ,
And the AH ….
Of awaiting ,
Within the last breath ,
Until I flow ,
Into your infinity ….

Winter 2007

"Happy New Year"

Congratulations !
Happy New Year ; Salute …..

The children burn in pain ,
Our monkey leaders have gone insane ,
God put them all in a chain ….

Ah , deeds without thought , so many words ,
Full of body , but no brain ….
The heart is pounding , but all blood in vain .
Life without love is such a shame …

Congratulations !

Hoora ,
Happy New Year ;

This year ,
The broken jointed weary hands
Which with one finger you command
Shall weave the chains upon your feet
From gold all so pure

Congratulations !

Happy new year ,

You are dying
But no need to fear ,
You shall buy the magic cure …..

Congratulations !

Happy New Year ; salute

And tell me ; who the hell shall tame
You who put your words , on the wall
Within a frame ….
Oh lord ;
Like wild beasts and priests ,
They roam around .
And in your name they loot all the ground ….

They dry the earth of all it's juice
As if it were a whore ….
Their greed indeed ,
Alike your love is endless forevermore

Yes , it seems
As if we are living in a crazy dream….

Yes , it seems
Not even the lord can tame
You who put your words within a golden frame …

Tell me ;
What religion , what God , what race …
Is the cause of this disgrace ?!

Tell me now :
Yes you , who in glory lead !
Don't hide your untouched face
Behind your Dollar shield !

Tell me who the hell is to blame
For these children , for this earth
That burn aflame ?!?!

Congratulations ; Hurray , Happy New Year ; Salute

Humanity has gone mad ,
From inside within ,
Drink in hand , on your screen ,
How does it seem ….

Adjust the color , that blood looks too green !

Yes , how does it seem ,
From outside within
Watch the numbers and news stream by ,
With that shameless shitty grin !

In the gutter ,
In the slum ,
So lifeless , so numb …
Always searching for a crumb
Beware , don't look down here   ,
For me you've made a nook down here
What the hell do you want to do down here …
From blood and shit ,
We'll make you a crown down here ,
Tell me ; what the hell you want down here ,
You bitch ,
You'll drown down here ,
Maybe you also want to lick my crumbs ,
Upon your face is where I want to cum !

You're a especial kind of breed ,
A reputed parasite who feeds ,
On others' desperate needs !
Yes , although I'm not bad with words ,
But you Sir , I can't describe indeed !

But you cultivated bastard , you fool ,
I think they didn't teach you this in school ;
The arms of these trees that grow from the seeds of hate ,
You have planted deep within this earth ,
Shall choke you like burning lead ,
Until all life from your body sheds !
Yes with these bitter seeds of hate ,
What else can be your fucking fate ?!

Congratulations ; happy new year ; my brother

We are created from love ,
Why should we suffer ?
You have a knife ?
Don't cut off my head ,
Bring it out to cut this loaf of bread !

You have got a big gun ,
Drop it , you have a bigger heart ..
We are all humans , we are all one !

And yet you still ,
Your own kind you want to kill ?!

Look at us , we are so alike ,
We are the same species and exact same kind …
Biology , feature , and feel all the same …
Something is wrong up here , yes , with the mind !

Yes , my brother ,
My heart is wrenched for every pain you suffer !

Look at the earth and sky ,
No jet you make like a bird can fly …
No bullet can move at the speed of sound ,
Yes , look closely , look all around ,
No bomb you make can match the sun ,
Let us come together and shine beneath it's rays as one !!

You on me , and me on you ….
It's just a piece of God Damn land ,
To own it in blood should we wash our hands ?

It's just some fucking paper cash ….
You want it , go ahead , jump on it ,
And make your stash !

But not so fast ,
Your intentions you shall never surpass ,
With this speed you're bound to crash !

I want to go on top ,
Of the highest mountain high ,
And put all of my soul and heart ,
Within a roaring thunder scream ,
That like an arrow from my body can depart ….

That it can shake the universe ,
Go up to God , down to the devil ,
Circle the earth and sky ,
Smoother then any jet can fly ,
Faster than any bullet ,
More explosive than an atomic bomb ,
With a blast ,
Like 10,000 tons of dynamite ,
That can forever enlighten this filth drooling night !

A deep desperate cry so loud ,
It would stir up this savage fighting crowd :

"Ah listen ;

You who are white , yellow , tan , or black …
The light of love shines through all cracks …
What ever holy book is your kind belief ,
Our God within is one , this is the real relief !

We must be quick ,
We need punctual intellectual improvisation ,
We need fresh vast vision ,
To create a universal religion !

Your movement and motions ,
Have intrigued my contemplation ,
From your temples standing high
To your vast devastation .
And I hereby summarize ,

All of your vast desires ,
The eastern winds and southern fires ,
All of the force of your biceps and hands
All of your God's strict commands ,
All of this fucking earthly mess
Within a tender kiss and caress !

You who live in a mansion , castle , or shack ….listen ;
Our lives , yours and mine ,
Are mere drops in this endless sea of history …
Any moment lived in hate ,
Is an utter waste of breath
Maybe we don't share the same life
But believe me we share the same death !

No matter who we are , where we live ,
How much we have , what we take and give
No matter what we lose and save ,
Our final home is all the same ; the grave ….

But what we do upon this earth ,
Is all that counts …
Our memory in good or in bad ,
In the hearts and minds of man ,
Shall flow and stay …
The more intense our deeds ,
The longer it will take to fade away !

Remember Hitler ,
How can anyone forget his hate ….
Although with it now I'm sure no one can relate !

Remember Edison , and Graham and Bell ,
How they eased our burden in fascination   ,
Their tale for generations we will tell   !!

And our great poets :

Hafez , and Mullana ,
Shakespeare and Poe ,
All lined within a row ...

To enrich the mind of man and give him vision ...
To create , to innovate , and most of all to love
To find himself and his mission !

The love of God was vibrant and alive ,
In all their hearts , and minds ,
In their words and works and strive !

You'll live to be a 100 the most ,
And yet with your gold and guns you boast ,
And God damn it , this I do not understand at all ;
That to the death of your own kind how can you toast ?!?!

Upon this earth you shall never find ,
A creature so ignorant , as man , to kill his own kind .

No creature or being upon this earth
Just due to sheer greed ...nor even plain need ,
Will destroy the earth ; their own habitat ;
Where they must eat , sleep , and breed !

Drop all arms , and come within my arms ,
How can love do harm ?
How the hell can you not care ,
Time and life is passing by ,
It's a pity for us not to share !

Oh God , Oh Lord , Oh Ahoura Mazde , Oh Allah
Or whatever they call you blah . blah , blah ,
Give us just one more chance ,

To make a humane stance ….

Please take us back from the very start ,
And take away all hate from within our hearts .

Put me back within a cave ,
I do not want this mansion ,
It has become my grave !

I don't need these vulgar flying lights ,
So calm and tranquil is the pure night !

I don't need this shitty poly-shirt …
Cover my body with your cotton buds ,
And your soft rich dirt !

I don't need this smoke-tank car ,
My lion head stallion ,
With 2 mouth sacks of hay ,
Can take me across the canyon ,
                                away ,
                                        distant far .

Take away this lingerie and loveless lace ,
With so much color , don't cover your precious face !

Like an animal so untamed ,
Who's just learning to play the game ….
Give me skin for skin ,
From outside within ,
Give me beat for beat ,
To flicker my heat .
Give me inch for inch ,
My thirst to quench .
Give me your everything and all ,
With no limit nor ration ,
Burn me from head to toe ,
Cover me with your engulfing passion .

We know no words , your tender touch ,
More than a novel , more than this poem ,
Can tell so much !

Oh Lord , take us back at least 10,000 years ,
When for power , greed , nor lust …
We would shed vicious tears !

Ah , yes , I know that this awakening scream ,
Is just a wild drunken dream .

How the hell can we untangle this fucking mess ,
With just a simple kiss and caress .

Ah , Silent , after 40 years or so ,
Your still just like a little boy ,
Who likes to play with his words ,
Like a toy of joy!

I have told you a 100 times or more ,
From these beings , Love , how you dare implore ?!?!

Silent , you 40 year old boy , till silence grows upon you forevermore ,
Telling the tale of love and life to fools ,
Is like washing the manure of mules !

*   *   *   *

With these words ,
Some may get the feel of steel ,
Some may giggle with joy ,
And play with their banana toy ,
Yet even if it takes more than many years ,
To bring down loving tears ,
From the sun of someone's eyes ,
And from their stamped mouths

Bring out cease-fire cries ….
From within their every grain of flesh ,
I shall live afresh !
Of death I shall have no fear ….from my core …
As within those tearful cries ,
Heart to heart , mind to mind , mouth to mouth ….
I shall live forevermore !

05/01/2009 Tehran

" More Lovingly"
                                          For Shahla ; of course

The sparkle in your eyes
Is from the Bubbling of which virgin springs
That wash me all so pure
That I see my clear reflection
Kiss the earth in the love of creation .

The honesty of your hands ,
Is merciless and thirst soothing ,
And the two torches of your tears ,
Illuminate the sorrowful tulips ,
Of your gardens of compassion ,
Like flaming fireflies .

From infringing borders ,
From the darkest horizons
From the farthest corners,
I will bring you all that is kindness :
God's most precious gifts ;
With the wings of passion ,
So that within these gliding moments ,
You may forever adrift .

Upon your wavy hair
I will hang the wildest of flowers…
Till you forget all that they cultivate
To hate ….

A piece of bread , a kiss ,
And a promise of reunion shall be enough
Sadness of a love and the yearning of a body

A caress and a companion shall be enough ....

This is not youth , this is the truth !
This is not the babbling of a midnight fever ....

This is forever.
This is the most ancient love
Within heart of the volcanic mountains
That has started to pound within my breast ...
This is why I scream ,
As if within a gasping dream
At last I know shall explode ,
This burning load ,
Within my scorching chest !

Oh ; it is like I never existed ....
Like I have evaporated upon the eastern winds ....
Like a body and face
That gradually fades ,
Within long bleeding minutes ,
Within tick-tock trickling moments ,
Within brief decaying decades ,
In the sharp turns of a long winding road ....

I no longer know
When I stayed ,
When I departed ,
When I was gone ;
I have sung a more lovely song ....

May 2002 .....Mashhad – Iran

"The Arising"

Again for Shahla

I hear my life ,
Trickling off ,
The secondhand ,
Pacing in the dense silence of the night ,
With a hollow tone .

My bread ,
Crumbles like my molded words ,
And my outworn book of poems ,
Is my prison .

O you ,
Who your veins ,
Guide my destiny ,
And your hands ,
Speak of hardship .
Your gaze ,
Is the meaning of gravity ;

Bring me down ,
From the height ,
Of my lost lacerated flight ,
To kneel ,
And to cry upon myself
To heal ;
This rough aching earth …
- With the words I have learned
In childhood .

Autumn 2007 Karaj

"Lovingly"

And again for Shahla

Courageous laughers of awakening ,
A touch of urgency ,
And caresses of emergency .
Greetings of the substance of sunshine ,
And tears of the elements of dawn ,
A body with the scent of paradise ,
And galaxy kisses arise ….

Winter 2007 Karaj

"Fate"

Your thousand fathers ,
Will not shed a tear
Upon your corpse ,
Rejected by the burnt soil .
You , who your smell ,
Even corrupts the atmosphere of hell .

You hacked off blossom heads ,
And raped the stars of their dignity ?
Let the sun ,
Now bake your buttery skin ,
For the royal feast of the raptors .

Do you hear ?
This is not the sound of mourners ,
Behind your inflated cadaver ,
It's the lustful invasion of the black vultures ;
Their beaks foaming and ,
Their eyes inflamed , roaming ,
Jubilant drunk ,
Saturated ,
From the scent ,
Of your fried fat flesh   .

And within a century moment
Your thousand perverse whore-faced fathers ,
Shall all come together ,
To share ,
Your mother ,
Before your bulging eyes .

Tehran – November – 2007

"Upon the lips of every Stranger"

I have spread my wings ,
Upon the storms ;
Soaring ,
A peak astounding ,
And a wave of winds binding ,
And a collapsed landing ,
Dazed , with a thunder roar .

I have been like this ,
From day one ;
The same man you see on every corner ,
Broke battered pure ,
With clinched fists of demand ,
Around the collar band of fate .

I have chanted the last verse
From the start ,
And when searching for my mother ,
Alley to alley ,
Eye to heart ,
Mind to mouth ,
I heard my name
In the eyes of every whore ,
And I found myself ,
Upon every stranger's lips .

Summer – 2007 Tehran

"Golden Thoughts"

Your flourishing wealth-house ,
Has taken the color of shit .
O you ,
Willing to grant a head ,
To bury your hands in the golden radiance ,
Of your master's excrements .

The Hah-Ho and bustle ,
The smoke ,
And the honking hustle ,
Of the early morning ,
Pumps the tired bloodworms ,
Into your veins .

The proportion of your body ,
Has become intertwined ,
Approach the mirror ,
Undress ,
Attempt to determine and define ,

Pull your drawers over your head   ;
Have mercy upon us ,
The stench of your mind ,
Is coming out of our nose .

Autumn 2007 Tehran

"Sunk"

You said :
"With this heart that you have ,
Full of blood so black
Full of filth , full of crack
You must have a vast off-loading port....I bet...."
I have worn out 10 leather boots on this path ,
In wrath ,
And nothing in sight , nothing yet !

You said :
"With this soul-rooted pain
You have all so real my friend .
You need 10 barrels of potent boiling wine ,
To sooth , at least , a bit , to heal my friend ."
I have drunken up the 20th
Without relief , a moment , until the end !

They have farted upon my mind ,
And with this heart they have half eaten ,
Emotions and sensations
How the Hell can I feel ,

They have pissed on my eyes ,
And thrown their Statistics
My destiny , number by number , grain by grain
At my graceless stone-aged face .
But my balls are made of steel ,
Yet I stand ,
With such an empty creel ...

Each day in front of the mirror
I make 12 daily faces for myself ,
With my own authentic sign and seal .

And I have made myself content ,
With this shit-drooling pen ,
That is running with no self-intent….!

I stare at my own shit
Like I stare at my book of poems ...
I'm not to blame ,
The most beautiful inspirations
Flow through the passage of my mind ,
When I'm oozing out my wastes of chrome !

Winter 2007 Tehran

"Conquered"

My rage ,
Dancing ,
In the spinning winds of freedom .

*****

For the rights of a human being ,
For the orphan ,
Born with me ,
Feeble and fledging .

For the tear ,
Implanted within my heart ,

Encrypted by the hands of my forefathers ,
The scroll of admiration and envy ,
Embedded in the soul of my nation ,
With an epic sword , long ago a century .

And now ,
The bulging gaze ,
Of hungry eyes ,
Upon the bare body of my mother .
And shame seeping
From my burning blurry eyes .

Summer 2009 Evin Prison

"For the Mourning for our Nation"

Like the awakening whispers of a wiser elder ,
From deep within a well ,
Life has thought me silence

****

O you shameless generation ,
Thou have broken all mirrors .
Your existence inspires hatred ,
In worldwide tremors .

My bewilderment is from these teeth marks ,
On my bread lost hand ,
And the faces of these human likes .

I know not ,
The violent breath ,
Of which evil horn-headed giant ,
Has casted such a blizzard season
Of lingering memory death
Upon our land   .

A season of plunder and prostrate perversion ,
A baffling season of contradictive conversion .

This is ,
Our city ,
With it's sedating acetous dust ,
It's whore-born rulers ,
Riding hard upon it's worn torn rump ,
With incising endless lust .

Alas ,
A hesitation ,
A mere moment ,
For contemplation ….
Our roots are deep within blood ,

Oh , Lord !
How we need , bad ,
A man
A hatchet
A hand !

*****
Like the calm whispers ,
Of a wiser elder ,
From deep below within ,
Life has thought me silence ….
Or….ah….yes….
Forgetfulness …..

Summer 1999 Evin Prison

"Conundrum"

A black , silent , heavy cloud
Has thrown it's weight upon our region .

Mind-quaking blasts ,
At the price of bread ,
For the children of Baghdad .
A blood clotted carpet ,
Stretching from Basra to Kabul .
Swords and machine guns ,
Have disturbed the long line of clowns in Beirut .
And the haze twisters of the southern deserts ,
Have tousled the beard of Uncle Sam .

In the courtyard ,
Of which wise man of Najaf ,
Should I recite this riddle ?
Before the feet of which world wandering fortuneteller ,
Should I throw the stars of fate   ?

In the year ,
That they sold off
The girls of the tribe ,
For a bag of flour .
For the yellow tear ,
That trickled because of gold .
For the athirst smile ,
That passed by meat .
And for animal faced leaders ,
Who are better off living within caves ,
Who never have a drop in their eyes ,
And are standing hard in prayer ,
On the back of the world ,
And have long said farewell ,
To emotions and thought ;

Has their God truly commanded this hellfire ?!?!

Summer 2007 Tehran

"Load"

The competition is severe ,
Sharpen your horns ,
And stay near .

Polish and shine your saddle ,
Make it shake ,
Make it rattle .
Stand by the side of the road ,
Maybe tomorrow ,
Another sultan will descend upon you :
God's most precious load .

Winter 2007 Karaj

"Temptation"

You have been left , alone ,
With the killer temptation of death .
Until satin blows you within his pipe .

And two smoking ghosts ,
Emerge from your body ,
To engage in a magical dance ,
Before your eyes , in trance .

Kiss my forehead ,
And praise my death intense in advance ,
For my God will always be afloat ,
In your enlightened caress .

Autumn 2007 Tehran

"Heavenly caress"
For my daughter : Dawn

Your innocent glance ,
Nails me to my cross of sins nakedly .
O you ,
The last reflection of my fertile beliefs .

Your tear is like radiant dew ,
The lone star of my roaming desert ,
That trickles upon my rippled crust lips ,
So that I arise again ,
To began my search ,
For the threshold of the first house of mirrors .

The smile of your first dawn ,
Was my last cry ,
For I knew ,
That the most everlasting love ,
From the creation of God ,
Had been breathed into you ,
Through an angelic spirit .

And the demon of our home ,
Has gone into peaceful rest ,
With your tender heavenly caress .

Autumn 1999 Evin Prison

"In Mourning"

For Mehdi Akhavan Salis
Who I can not say a word about

Oh your words ,
More lethal
Than the poison ,
Conspired into the goblets
Of the never-surrendering warriors .

The mystery of fiery hearts ,
Who has shared with you so warmly ,
That you've incinerated all our minds ,
O your reflective rendering existence ,
Upon our blurred baffle of these times
A smile ,
Broken and bitter ;
In image and subsistence .

*****

You said yourself ,
That there is a place ,
Far beyond all boundaries ,
Where the burnt-love elders ,
Come together ,
Gracious and unyielding ,
To grant flaming spirits of vintage passion ,
And narcotics of untainted compassion ,
To us the rebellious ,
Encaged within our rage ,
All in abundant boundless rations ,

And there will be dust-swirling stumping ,
With jubilant sighs of freedom ,
And crazed chain-ripped romping
From their potent purity ,
And soul-searching butterflies
Upon exemplary extinct floral buds ,
So unique in color , form , and sensation ,
Within this wild garden of raving lovers ,
Is a soothing uproar of ornamentation ,
And the dance of the maidens ,
Of the wind and fire ,
Is as if tranquil peace ,
Has prevailed within all desires .
Oh you said it yourself ….

I departed from myself ,
My brain intact ,
To travel upon your plains and mountains ,
To journey beyond your forests and deserts ,
To drink from the eternal fountains
To taste your nights' extract .
For there is within me ,
A seed of pain ,
So pure ,
I will not in any kind of soil ingrain ,
Damn your deep implant   .

So many nights ,
I surpassed without light ,
Nor wine to sip .
So much dry bread ,
Within my heart's blood ,
I dipped .

Before the cavemen police ,
Down my throat I swallowed ,
The pride and nostalgic dignity ,

Of the great immortals so hallowed ,
That I vomit up like this to follow :

Damn it man ,
I have gone insane ,
From my kin and relations ,
Only scars of infested wounds remain
And from my faith ,
Only hatred and devastation ….
So diversely profane ;
They stamped me upon my forehead ,
As so profoundly Godless ,
Immoral without shame ,
Condemning my life and death .
They've thrown so many sharp stones
At my head …
That I've become blitzed , so numb my brain
Seeking the doors of a welcoming wine-house ,
Graveled in throbbing pain .

Oh , don't say it ,
I know you said it yourself !
But Damn , if you must be like this ,
For under the dragon ,
You had hidden the treasure ,
Yourself in loneliness .

******

Oh you God-seekers ,
You revolt-speakers ,
Laying legs up ,
warm
Within your harems
Behold a man ,

Free of all above , below and before .
Oh your enduing and incisive existence ,
Upon our despise and moaning ,
A smile ,
Broken and bitter ,
In vision and substance .

"Beamish"

For my self-sacrificing mother-in-law

From past to present ,
Year to year ,
Fear after fear ,
Nothing has changed .
Only the roads ,
Upon the wrinkles of your leather-like skin ,
Have twisted into turns ,
Ending where they begin .

Your eyes narrate the suffering of the centuries ,
That take me to the battlefields of long ago .
And your arms are truly immune to hatred ,
Although you have always carried your beloved dead ,
Upon your enduring shoulders .

From past to present ,
You have cried in dissent ,
From this throat clogging chunk of bread .

O Mother ,
I thought I heard your cry ,
Twirling towards the sky :
"Oh Lord ,
I will not forgive you ,
Ever again ! "

Summer 2008

"The Sheikh of Palm trees and Oasis"

Back and before ,
Never forward forevermore .
Reverse and rewind ,
Swirling up and around ,
Ascending higher to the highest ,
To find a matter of your own kind ,
Yet grasping all that is emptiness ,
Fond to be found .
Descending down ,
Back to attack ,
On the ground ,
Yet still all that is nothing ,
To be found .

Back to the age of the great ,
And forward to your current ,
Checkmate fate   .

A broken vision forming ,
In disarray ,
Of the killer temptation ,
Of love and humanity ,
Within your destructive imagination .

In a millennium moment ,
The earth and sky ,
Changed places ,
In roaring rotation ,
To playfully punish one another's destiny ,
In avenged devastation .
With God and Satan ,
Switching their thrown location .

Oh our Sheikh of the palm trees and oasis ,
With your ladies' panties ,
In your hand ,
As your flag ,
And your iron cast book upon your face ,
Like a mask tightly braced .

If you were here to see ,
How your tale of erotic orgies ,
With heavenly nymphs so divine ,
Whose ripe bursting breast
Trickle honey and milk , and wine
Has immersed ,
These crippled cane in hands ,
Into immense rivalry ….
Oh you would have loved to see ,
This commotion of demand .

And to have tasted ,
With your own eyes ,
The poisonous cut ,
Of your mirror sword ,
In the centre ,
Of the round mass of time .

Oh you idiot of the ages ,
Nothing ,
Not even your soul ,
Rests till eternity .
Yet everything breathing and all ,
Crumbles with the passing of time ,
Grain by pain ,
Disintegrating to fall ,
And then restructuring again ,
Gradually grain in restrain
Transforms within a circular vision ,
Incurs conviction ,
Regenerating again to rotate in reiteration .

And this temptation ,
Of never and forever ,
Is endless .

Winter 2008 Karaj

"Dizzy Earth"

The Moon :
A grave gray curse .

The Sun :
A red quibbling smile of burning hope .

The Wind :
The narrator of forbidden tales .

The rain :
Desperate salty tears of the Gods .

Freedom :
A deceit of mocking irony .

Love :
A dark violet envy .

The human :
Valued by the kilo .

The Lord :
Loaned in the Euro .

And you are the self-destructive being ,
Obliviously standing ,
In the centre of this fart waste earth ,
Capsized from all of this ,
Not knowing why ,
You didn't open your eyes to cry ,
A lot earlier or a bit later
Within this mad haste earth .
Ah this earth ... ,
This double sugar paste earth …..
Winter 2007 Tehran

"Full"

The scent of rain and gun powder ,
Is flowing from the night's mouth .
The sky is wrinkled ,
In the gravity of it's intense frown .
Your feet upon the warm ashes of earth ,
And the envy of a dissolving love ,
Extruding through your throat's cove .

Winter 2008 Karaj

"Death of Dawn"

In mourning of my eternal
master Ahmed Shamloo

The tears of dawn bloomed ,
The wings of a scream ,
From deep below within ,
Infringe the known horizon .
Do you know the occasion of the hour :
The dark ritual of time   ;
The chanting of songs ,
For the mourning of our unknown lover ,
In broken rhyme ?

"Upside down"

The best time of my life ,
Is entrapped within a broken frame .
My most bitter hours ,
Are spinning ,
In the twists and turns ,
Of your enchanting dance .

My mouth was needless of words ,
And my heart needless of kisses ,
When you ran the world ,
With your almond eyes ,
Upside down before me .

Damn these tears ,
And Damn their creator .
Damn these hands ,
That only weave the rug of distance .

Spring 2008 Tehran

"Value"

Living in a land ;
Where the Mullah's kebabs are more expensive ,
Than the value of your life !
Where grave digging ,
Provides the best employment opportunity .

Look into yourself ,
Look all around you will see ,
You have no where to plea ,
Your freedom now lays ,
In the force of the knuckles ,
Of these sky pounding hands !

Summer 2009

"Our making of Love"

Two explosions of love face to face ,
Shooting star-like sparks ,
Into the endless night of space .

The vibrations of electrons ,
In ecstasy and anguish ,
Surging to collide
Upon the surface of our mélange bodies .
Gently breaching the boundaries of pleasure .

Our making of love ,
This is how I define upon ,
Forever this fading earth ,
To shine upon .
From the unknown beginning ,
To the crowning end ….
A silent kiss , a deep embrace .

Winter 2005 Tehran

"Unknown"

Love , a burning envy .
Freedom , a feared delusion .
Our people , the significance of numbers .
Our art , valued by the kilo
Our God , sold in the Euro
Our differences , a bewildering confusion .
And yet upon our ignorance
We have so easily reached a mutual understanding !

Winter 2001 Tehran

"Silent Scream"

In the warmth of our shelter
We sleep
A deep conscious sleep .

Upon these nights ,
We are at times awakened by a conscientious fright .

The dripping drops
That drip
Drip
Drop

The drops that pace
The silence in a hallow tone ,

The drops that fill the stagnant space
With a silent scream .
To awake us from our deluded dreams !

The drops that cry ,
Drip
Drip
Why ?!

The drops that bleed
Tric
Tric
Trickle

The drops that pace
The silence in a hallow sound
The drops with no desire
Other than to wash away the unholy filth of our ground .

The drops that

Drip
Drip
Bleed
Our seeds of love to feed .

That drops that cry

Tric
Tric
Trickle

The drops
That pause the night
With a silent glow ;

Come
Open
Open
My flow !!

1992 Tehran

"The Journey"

And again and again for Shahla

Throw free the coolness of your lustrous hair upon my face ;
I want to taste the mountain dew of the farthest water falls .

Can't you see ,
My crusty lips ,
And my body burning in hallucinating fever .

Sacrifice floral scented kisses to me ,
I want to taste the extract from the buds of the firstborn springs .

They have camouflaged our bread ,
In the depths of filth .
Do you know the pain ,
Of writing from love ,
With hands so stained ?
Not relinquishing a lid ,
Till the light of dawn ,
For the suffering of your own kind ,
Yet lonelier than the wind ,
Forsaken from behind .

What can I say ,
The dust upon my rusty skin ,
Speaks for me itself .
I didn't find ,
I didn't taste ,
A drop of that eternal lucid crystal ,
What can I do ,
If I've no shame of my pure words ,
From the sparkling fountain of my mind .

Come and let us cry together ,
The last survivors of love ,
For there is no other sign remaining ,
Of purity and innocence .
In these fierce fields of flesh hungry predators ,
With your eyes and caress ,
With your nakedness ,
Invite me to the delicate feast
Of virginity and finesse .

I know ,
There's no longer a torch ,
Nor a clear path ,
Nor the sheltering shadow of a lone tree ,
Nor a sigh , a cry
From near or distant ,
Nor a whisper of a drying stream in persistence .

Everything that is of love ,
Has long died in our land ,
Our glance we must expand
Beyond the barren plains
Of this darkness spreading domain .

1999 Summer Tehran

"Love Walk"

For the imprisoned hikers

To journey ,
With love
Infringing all borders ,
Farther than all known horizons ,
Surpassing the earth's circular corners .
With relentless passion .

Hiking upon the equator ,
Upon the human divide ,
If only your curiosity could see ,
Beyond the boundaries of mankind ,
And your compassion in shelter ,
You could hide …..
Witnessing their self-destructive ignorance ,
You raised your arms in full courage ,
To surrender without resistance ,
From the other side .

Maybe in fear of their own hearts ,
They placed a blindfold upon you ,
As the earth's grace ,
Through your eyes shined .

Ah…you surrendered to your compassion ,
Long before they took you captive .

Now come kneel by my side ,
By the river my friends ,
And let us cry together ,
For the oblivion of our own kind .
November -2010 – Tehran

My Grandmother's tale of :
ADAM AND EVE

One night I asked my grandmother ,
In the depths of childish intrigue ;

"Grandma ; why do I love all the nature so much ,"
That the creations and wonders I yearn to touch ?"

She replied with her tender voice ,
That from 95 years of age ,
Had grown slightly coarse

My kind hearted beloved son ,
A tale I must tell you before my life is done ,
Until you realize where you stand ,
By the seas , mountains, and the lands .

But first please close the window ,
As it is getting cold ,
My bones are weak ,
As I am 95 years old !

"In the beginning of creation ,
Adam roamed the earth ,
All so lonely ,
Searching a friend ,
A companion , as he was the only .

He searched , searched , and searched ,
Until he reached the gracious mountains so high ,

So high that they almost touched ,
The endless sky .

So full of life and color ,
From low to peak .
For his joy and love ,
Nowhere else he would need to seek .

His desperate soul yearned in mirth ,
As he heard the wild eagle cry ,
As if calling him to come join and fly ,
And in spirit he sensed rebirth .

And the rivers ,
That through the mountain side ,
Entangled , to glow and shine ,
So crisp , so clear , so refined .
With so much current grace ,
That in their bright twinkling ,
He could have sworn ,
He saw the Almighty's face ,

He fell in love with the mountain highs so deep ,
His heart within his chest , he could no longer keep !

From his chest he took his inflamed throbbing heart ,
And like an arrow his life to depart ,
Threw it far to the mountain top ,
With all of his mortal strength ,
In that burning moment on the spot ,
There and then dead he dropped ,
To free his soul , love , and life in synch .

God looked down ,
With a very sad frown ,
And in the hesitation of a brief moment ,
That for us could have lasted a 1000 years ,
In hazy torrents ....

An instant so intense , so deep so refined
With our mortal minds , we can not define .
God commenced to contemplate ,
To see what he would do with Adam's fate .

He thought , thought , and rethought ,
For a solution to the survival of his creation he sought .
Forward and back , round and round ,
To cipher in a sphere ,
His long waited plan to adhere .

He then decided to return Adam's heart ,
Within his breast ,
And let him sleep in peace ,
As upon his journey
He would need a rock bottom rest .

To survive and strive , to thrive ,
He gave him another chance ,
To see his wonders ,
And grasp his boundless love within a glance .

After two days of three ,
From his sleep he gently awoke ,
In a daze , his heavy head
With inflated hands to stroke ,

He looked all around ,
Up to the endless pure blue heavens ,
Down on the green grass ground .

Again he realized that he was all so lonely ,
And then in a severed minute of torrent torture ,
His soul in sorrow sank without a sheer sound !

Of course ,
As love and need always find their coarse ,

After an hour or two in remorse ,
He regained his will ,
Not to sit lifeless still ,
The voice of his relentless desire ,
In his mind ,
Burned in the tongues of a blazing fire ,

His determination up-roaring like a wild thunder storm ,
Within his veins and beseeching brain ,
In his soul and heart and every breathing grain ,
And yet like the endless night space ,
That hollow drops could pace ,
It was so calm , so tranquil , so eternal mute !
Like a firm fearless courage so resolute ,
So armored solid , so immortal , so acute .

With an unyielding fatal faith
So rock rigid , so solid bold ,
That in a moment he assumed he could forever hold ,
The ancient love
Pounding within the rough rugged mountain chests ,
In his untamed brisk beating breast !

Again with his red vibrant heart ,
And his spirit so bravely enlightened ,
He commenced to depart .

With his thirst so rich , so alive
So vibrant his thrive ,
Ascertain that he was the man ,
His will and passion not a sham .
To set foot upon his solitary sacred quest ,
To discover and embrace ,
Heart to heart , beat to beat

In flesh , face to face ,
To put his inherited divine love to the test ,
To find the truth ,
And leave behind all the rest .

To keenly find , his own kin and kind ,
Again he set foot upon the path of his naked quest …

After four days or three ,
He reached a sparkling sea of ample blue .
He gazed in a bewildered daze ,
Upon the torrent shining waves ,
So profoundly rich in color and motion ,
It could virtually inspire any unearthly notion !

He could ponder upon no other way ,
But to watch , and stay , in joyous emotion .
Bedazzled in this tremendous abyss of purple blue ,

In prompt ,
He again lost his heart
And went abruptly insane ,

The flames of love again started to flow ,
In raging pain of lava slow ,
Within his eager burning veins !

In utter agony he yearned ,
To embrace with all of his strength ,
The rich bright waves within his arms so immortally tight ,
So that his soul with that ocean blue may unite !

Than he beheld in amazement to be shook
As he closely took a look ,
At a radiant rainbow ,
That had begun to form ,

Upon the vast horizon ,
So vivid in shades of brilliant chrome ,
As if a colorful gift , adrift ,
From the sky ,
To that sea of vast entity ….
Shining upon that sheer calm blue ….

Illuminating the slashing tides ,
That behind soft ripples ,
Would astound to hide ,
In gliding tones of contrast and harmony ,
Within this mutual sea and sky color symphony ,
So vibrant and alive ,
To dance and strive
They would play in rays of accord and strife ,
As colors truly are the essence of life .

He knew in a abiding moment of hesitation ,
All so brief ,
What he must do ,
To find true relief .

His love for that boundless sea ,
Was so pearl pure ,
That to his anguish ,
He could find no other sailing cure .

His aching bird heart full of red wine blood ,
Startled , beating fiercely , imprisoned
Within the white walls of this quaking chest .
As he could not resist for a second more ,
Upon creation's vast virgin shores ,
To allow his passion to run in lead ,
He grasped with all the power
He could summon to plead ,
His wreckage-bound heart , anchor freed

And with all of his inherited Almighty's might ,
Threw it wildly into the fading horizon
Where the sinking sun had just met the sea ,
In a light of a unique intimate embrace ,
With colors colliding to contour a new form of grace .

Yes , with his own bare hands ,
He threw his inflaming heart ,
With all of his anguished might ,
Into the sunset mélange horizon ,
Till it was no longer in clear sight !

Again in a flash of fleet light ,
His spirit from his body gained height ,
His flesh Still burning in crimson bright ,
From the flames of his passion yet not extinguished ,
Yet the embers of life to his love he had relinquished .

Then upon the tanned sea shore sands ,
Like a heavy mass of ground bound lead
Arms spread open wide ,
To grasp that surging ocean ,
He dropped stone dead ,
His eyes still gazing in the horizon ,
Fixed straight ahead .

God glanced down ,
With a very desperate frown all so rumpled ,
So intense , so magnified ,
That in a moment it made the earth age and crumple .

He summoned his angels from throughout his realm ,
With a thunderous cry in command .
For their stark compassion he did demand .

The Lord's clamor , the universe it overwhelmed ,
So loud , so mind-quaking deep ,

Yet it was so gentle ,
It could really make you weep .

God's scream , shook the earth in restless tremors :
"Come" He exclaimed , "Come my beloved children ,
And with me in sorrow cry .
I am lost within my own creation ,
And I don't know why !

My Adam , My love ,
Can not survive ,
What must I conjure to keep him alive ?!

In contemplation of his creation ,
It took me 2 million years ,
And another million ,
To abandon my relentless fears .
In his flawless face ,
I invested all of my art and grace .
Within his soul ,
I breathed my love ,
From the purest elements of high above .

And in his spirit ,
I embedded instincts , and intuition , so refined ,
For him to distinguish and determine and define .
And I implanted within his roots and race ,
A never-ending hunger to flourish and thrive ,
To explore and discover and strive .

I assume ; I emplaced the burning love of my earth ,
Within his soul too exquisite extreme ,
That he was too eager to unite ,
With all the vivid nature in sight .

And he yearned too much ,
In blind rush ,
To feel and touch .

Yes ; now I think the love was too desperate deep ,
That his inflamed heart within his chest ,
He could no longer keep .

And yet maybe it is experience that he lacks ,
To keep his vital organ intact .

And though I am well aware ,
He needs a soul mate with whom to share ,
And in the flesh and blood of his own kind ,
Can he only feed ,
To plant mankind's reproductive seed .

Yes ; indeed , in the end ,
I know what I must do ,
But I really thought he could survive by himself ,
For at least a month or two !

Can't you see my dear angels ,
That within his adventures and quests ,
I am putting my own sacred wisdom to the test .

The Lord then released a gentle weary sigh in dismay ,
In waves of despair and disarray ,

His breath unleashed the untamed surging winds ,
To wildly soar ,
To entangle , entwine , and uproar .

Then after a blink hesitation ,
The angels in empathy began to cry ,
And rivers of pure diamond tears ,
Began to pour from the sky .

This glowing rapid of flow ,
With the up-heaving torrents
From the lord's torment grief and exhaled blow ,
Abruptly combined to form ,

The earth's initial rain storm .

The Lord in his solitude of discontent ,
Did not bother to yield the storm for a day or two ,
Until he saw that it may cause drastic harm ,
Then with a slight motion of his right arm ,
He dispersed the clouds ,
And the sky gradually grew calm .

Then after another seven days or eight ,
The Lord again called upon his angels ,
For he was anxious , and could no longer wait .

In potent pure humbleness ,
The Lord consulted the angels ,
In his crisp coherent voice ,
And in praise of this modest gesture of the Almighty ,
The playful angels sang and danced in divine rejoice .

"Now my darlings" the Lord exclaimed ,
"Is not the time to applaud and acclaim "

I know who I am ,
No more , no less ,
Let us unravel this bitter mess .

"Give him one more chance
To make his final solitary stance "
The angels replied in their soft childish persuasive tone ,
Their innocence untarnished , their virtues never to be torn .
"Oh , Lord , let him gain his strength and competence ,
For upon his mission he will need his confidence .

This journey will help him later down the road ,
When he is conveying a crippling load .
Oh , Father , give him one more survival chance ,
To roam your earth in mirth ,
His passion and wisdom to enhance .
We are certain that in rebirth

With all the vigor of his inheritance ,
He will endure the lapse indeed ,
For you Lord to judge the quality in your creation ,
Of his rare breed . "

God without the slightest motion or sign of emotion ,
 Descended into a tranquil state of meditation .
In his heart he well knew ,
What Adam would eventually need ,
Yet he was conscious of the sheer destructive greed ,
Adam's seeds in time would grow and feed .

And the Almighty's conscience was like a volcanic mountain upon
his head .
As he was ascertain that humanity in abolishment would yield !

Then after a few moments all so brief ,
The Lord finally sighed with relief ,

"Fine" he concluded
"Bring me his heart to be replenished"
And after 5 seconds in fascination
God's work was finished .

He restored Adam's heart within his chest ,
And let him sleep ,
For to recover his vim he would need sea bottom rest .

In a days few ,
He would rise afresh to commence his quest ,
With the sparkling tears of the morning dew ,
And set foot upon his path anew .

Adam awoke to a radiant dawn , so crisp and clean
So sunshine fine , as if in a dream ,
The rays of light so densely bright ,
The colors so vivid , you could almost touch ,
Such a glorious dawn of this unique kind ,

Now upon the earth you will never find .
In our petty lives we could have never seen ,
A dawn so vibrant , so brilliant , so grass root green .

After all , it was the first days of creation ;
The air and sun so radiant pure
All pains it could really cure .

All the land's surface so vibrant , so full of life ,
You could almost hear the earth's face breath ,
And even the devil sighed with love ,
From deep beneath .

Yes my son ,
Now mankind has sucked the earth of it's vital juice ,
All so lifeless , all so blazing dry .
For just his sheer lust to possess .
I don't know why !

In his intolerance ,
Ignorance and destructive greed ,
The earth and sea ,
Shall forever bleed.

Ah my dear son ,
The pain is too lethal , it will not ease to heal
Until to the force of compelling love we all truly kneel .

The infected wounds of this earth ,
Are too fatal , too immensely great .
They will find no relief ,
Until we see ourselves and this earth as one ,
Within our firm beliefs .

Ah , the anguish runs too bitter deep ,
It is too heart-quacking great ,
Upon this case , for our survival ,
I am sure we can all relate .

Yet we must not ponder in remorse ,
We must let the healing find it's course .
We must not stray , nor in fantasy adrift ,
The earth from this unholy filth we must lift .

Our differences should enhance ,
The motion of the world ,
And make it spin round and round ,
In a wild stirring pace ,
That it will leave our heads in a bedazzled daze ,
Till we can see no colors , no country , nor race
And embrace each other as one in this emancipating haze .

Yes so abruptly fast , yet so smoothly round and round .
Till a loveless soul upon this earth can not be found .

If I could my son ,
I would squeeze down all of our holy books ,
Within a magic moment of trance ,
To only extract a friendly hand ,
A warm kiss and tender glance .

We only have one earth ,
One land , one sun ,
Let us come together and shine beneath it's rays as one .

The colors of all our skins ,
Can be found upon this earth within .
Who's bronze , yellow , black or white ,
We have all come from one shade of light ;
Let us all unite .

Who's orange , yellow , black , or tanned ;
The earth , the hills , the rivers , the stars and sand .

Come on ,
Open your eyes ,
All of these colors in harmony create our land .

If tan , white , pink , blue or black ,
The light of love shines through all cracks .

Oh , my son it really twists my age old heart to see ,
That mankind can only relate ,
Within their ignorance and burning greed .
You are young , your life all so full ahead indeed ,
But it seems for your future's sake ,
This rage for our extinct fading love ,
I can not fake .

Oh my son ,
I see that you are growing sad ,
With this sorrow enough we've had .

I am so sorry my dear , pardon me
I almost forgot the story .

Please forgive me as my senses are weary .
Kindly close the window gently ,
As it is getting bone shaking cold ,
After all please remember ,
That I'm 95 years old .

Yes please forgive me ,
Let us flow back like the rivers to the sea ,
To this never ending story .

Adam awoke to a brand new golden dawn ,
So vibrant , so clean , so robust green .
He rose to his feet swiftly ,
As to find his eternal love ,
He was so very keen .

The reflection of sunshine upon the morning dew ,
Glimmered a vivid light of bright hope within his eyes ,
And in an instant he so dearly knew ,

That upon this day ,
He would at last find a way ,
To find and grasp his relentless passion ,
The killer love that took his breath ,
The throbbing impulse ,
That had twice caused his death .
Implanted within him from high above ;
A force of immortal power so mighty ,
The essence of the creation of the Almighty ,
Of elements so flawless ,
So transparent clear ,
That to surrender all ,
One felt no fear ,
From the virgin springs of the heavens ,
So mind burning pure ,
That with a drop ,
All wounds it could cure .
An erupting inspiration ,
Engulfing like the infinite flames of the sun ,
And then Adam had the sudden urge to run .

To speak too much ,
Of this power I am sure ,
Will burn our mind , body , and tongue like manure .
Adam ran with the speed of sound ,
Till within a thick tranquil forest himself he found .

So peaceful , yet so living a place ,
All the life he wanted to embrace .

With colorful fruits ,
In sorts of all ,
From trees of large and small .

Such juice , such sweet tastes ,
He would love to eat in haste .

Ah , this life is so bitter sweet ,
With my mate I soon must meet .

I can almost smell her beastly body raw ,
Maybe there by the river I thought I saw .

He searched restlessly without a fuss
From breaking dawn to the sinking dust .

And yet the jungle was so rich in life and shade ,
That his loneliness soon began to fade .

"Oh , my Lord this nature has possessed me so unconscious deep ,
I doubt for a moment again I can sleep .

On the run , in hunt and hide ,
The wolves are always by my side .

From the massive elephant stance ,
To the exotic sounds of the wild bird dance .

From the fearsome tiger growl ,
To the glass of darkness ,
Shattered by the calm rhythm of the owl .

In this wilderness all play without care so free
Ah , the jungle is true democracy   ;

In this habitat night and day ,
I find myself in so many ways .
Ah , how immensely all the green ,
Flows within me from my soul's screen .

And ah , now with a glance at my ancestors ,
I reminisce so graphically ,
How from tree to tree ,
I swung as a proud prime monkey ,
And then in an evolving pace ,
Gradually my face ,
Gained a light of art and emotion ,
From the gentle touch of your grace .

Then step by step I began to see ,
A better way of living free ,
With my instincts all intact ,
I began to ration upon doubtless facts .

Your thought and mind ,
Can put you above the rest .
Knowledge is a true treasure chest .

I learned day by day ,
To cover my bareness ,
In a better way .

With my intuition ,
I discovered the magic aid of fire ,
But yet for much more than this burned my desires .

I learned with all of my love and devotion ,
To tend to my family's needs ;
Their body and soul ,
To nourish and to cherish , to feed ,
In a manner so tender fair ,
Even more than for myself ,
I could ever care ."

Adam returned to glance
The light of reality ,
As he emerged from this reflective trance .
To find himself and make his final stance .

"Oh , Lord , here even without my mate ,
I am so wild so free from all that is hate .
All the living colors ,
I can grasp within a glimpse ,
From the bright lustful red ,
To the parrot purple humming inside my head .
From the flashy sexy pink ,
To the nostalgic brick ,
From the liquid green ,

To the soothing mellow orange yellow ,
Of the age shedding willow .
 And the soft tranquil blue ,
That is so reflective true .

I have lost my tongue and sense of speech ,
In the twinkling of the leaves ,
No longer shall I ever roam ,
The jungle is my last and final home .

Ah , Lord , this love shall kill me again ,
Please this torment for a moment ease
This torrent rupture within my soul ,
Have mercy and seize .

And yet in a flash that is beyond all math ,
This wrath transcends to shivering delight ,
Back and forth on an elusive path .
With no friction at all or internal fight .

And in a trickle ,
My soul and brain ,
My body , my heart , my every grain ,
Is burning in joyous flames .

This love , so true , so rare so immortal pure
Only death seems to be the cure .

But Lord if at this very moment ,
I should die within a mere breath ,
I am so fully content and fear no death .

This unrequited love has brought me so much anguish ,
To this nature my heart I must relinquish ."

Adam's throbbing heart ,

Was pounding so solid hard , so restlessly
Like a wild animal within his chest .
And as he reached to grab it within his scorching breast
He had no chance to take it with his trembling hands ,
For his heart was so vibrant , so full of fresh radiant blood ,
That just with the simple intent ,
It broke through his ribs ,
And in the farthest corner of the jungle it flew and went ,
And with it his lower left rib upon a nearby tree was sent .

For a moment two or three ,
A dark dense silence sank upon the jungle ,
All so heavily .

Like the deceptive calm before the rage of a storm ,
Like a pause of truce in nature ,
For the lost to find shelter or their home .

Then in a blinding flash of light ,
His heart passed by in red flames , out of sight .

And in a moment without breath ,
All creatures heard his heart pounding still beyond ,
For there was no death .

The wild beating of his heart ,
Drew all the jungle still .
And it shook the four corners of the earth ,
Like God's monster drill .
For life in blood ,
His full hearted love could not kill .

Love can make the mountains dance ,
Hold the thunderous seas calm within a trance .
Love can really make you move ,
To the edge of your dreams you can grove .
With love there is no fear of death ,
No need for water , food , nor breath .

With true love ,
Within all hearts ,
You can live until infinity ,
Launch your love out to the universe ,
Love can only save humanity .

Oh , my Lord ,
Back to the story it's getting late .
I must rest as my age is great .

His heart was so alive ,
Working like a machine ,
But as it was pounding in the love of nature ,
It's blood was green .

And so much blood ,
It burst upon the trees and leaves from within .
For months to come it was spring in spring again .

In honor of Adam's love , so raw , so rare, so free
All the creatures lived in utter silence for two days or three .
To praise his love all so bare ,
His grief they would together share .

The angels prudently held their breath ,
Shaking in shock and fear ,
And they could not hold back their pearl tears .

In dread that the Lord would be angry with disgust ,
And they all mourned jumping up and down ,
So hard that it shook the foundations of the universe ,
Warp and weft .
And caused the moon to come upon the sun ,
The sun upon the moon right and left .

Then all the creatures within an astonished glimpse ,
Witnessed the first ever eclipse .

From his rest the Lord awoke ,
He was still weary ,
And his head he shook .

Calm down , my children ,
Let their be light ,
Without light there is no life ,
Let us all share the light .

If the sun does not shine for a moment three ,
All hell shall break loose , you will see .
And then the earth shall explode ,
Like a useless freezing load .

That is why my children ,
Who I so adore ,
I created one love , one light , one truth , one sun ,
From my core .
So that all could come together beneath it's rays as one ,
Endlessly forevermore .

The Lord looked down upon Adam ,
And in a moment of gentle hesitation ,
That for us could have been a 1000 years of fascination .

This moment in the heavens I can't explain my friend ,
My tongue and brain shall burn until the end .

Of such unearthly mind blazing emotions no one should speak .
No words , nor pictures , no low , nor peak .
This light will blind your eyes you can't behold ,

Shield your eyes , ears , and face
Stay alert , stay near , your body brace
From this fervent ray ,
And maybe behind the mirrors of your mind ,
The truth to this love one day ,
You may search to find .

After this brief pause and hesitation ,
The Lord let out a tender laugh ,
And before he went back to rest he knew ,
In the end what he would finally have to do .

The angels sighed with great relief ,
Jubilant in joy , compassion , and love
With their indestructible firm belief .
All for a half laugh all so brief .

All of this noise and commotion ,
Brought up the devil from his realm of doom and devotion .
Straight up to the Lord he went and knelt ,
And upon his feet he so gravely wept :

"Oh , my Lord ,
I long so madly much ,
For your tender touch .
I am only in love with you ,
Nothing less , nothing so , nothing such .

In your true love I have so much undiminished devotion ,
That I have accepted a life of sheer isolation . "
The Lord was full of mercy and compassion ,
He gently caressed his head ,
In the most loving fashion .

I can give you one more chance ,
To take back your vow of jealous hate and change your stance
In a few hours after I rest a bit more and clear my head ,
You shall behold my new creation ,
Behold in respect shall all the angels in complete fascination .

For the sake of the burning love within your chest ,
That has made you mad with hate ,
And will not let you rest .
If you want to be with me ,
Before Adam you must kneel ,
His beauty and grace you must praise ,

And back to my kingdom ,
From your black realm I shall raise .

The devil looked deeply with boundless affection ,
Into the Lord's eyes ,
And he knew as always to the Lord he could never lie :

"If you transform me to a million particles of dust ,
And upon the seas and earth you thrust ,
I shall only kneel to you ,
With this love there is nothing else I can do .

You're the only one I cherish and admire from my core ,
I shall love nothing less , nothing more .
And if I rot in the filth of hell for 3 billion years ,
The heat shall not dry my burning tears .

In my realm I shall not rest ,
To take away your love from his chest .

His head I will manipulate ,
In a haze of lust and greed ,
To daze doom his fate ,
Descending on the path of hate .

How can you love him more than me ,
He's not worthy of your love cant' you see .

Ask your angels ,
How can anyone dare compare ,
My love for you ,
I will not share . "

The Lord wanted to give him leave ,
But to stay with the lord for a few moments more ,
He did indeed ,
Sincerely beg and plead .

Alright your bare honesty is acknowledged and enjoyed ,

For a few hours more you may stay ,
At one time you were my best angel anyway .

I'll need you there for him to judge ,
To see and chose between gold and dust,
Between love and lust ,

Now the time has come for me ,
To make eternal history .

Although I know that in a few 1000 years ,
For some the earth will be living hell ,
But this is how I made my plan ,
To create all the lands ,
And now it is really out of my hands .

Now only mankind can guide his fate ,
To love and forgive , and be free from hate .
And I am certain that many will feed ,
Their destructive greed of power and gold ,
And with bitter sorrow their rampage I shall behold .
But of one thing I never thought I would find ,
Was that man could be so ruthless ,
To burn , kill , rape ,and destroy his own kind .
Yes of this potential brutality I had never thought ,
If so a solution I would have sought .

Any how four million years ago ,
This is how I planned the creation of man ,
The seas , skies , and land .
And now it is truly out of my hands .

It will really set my mind ablaze ,
As I observe within an obscene haze ,
How they play with lethal weapons like toys ,
And then pass them on to their girls and boys .

I'll grant them solid Iron ,

From the mountain hearts ,
To make tools to plow their fields ,
Yet instead they put it to the flame ,
To craft swords and battle-shields .

How they will dry the land of all it's juice ,
And their own daughters they seduce .
They will so happily exchange the bright green nature ,
With cold bricks , glass , and steel ,
That has no life and can not feel .

And how they will assume ,
That earth like their markets they can inflate :
The salty waters shall flow upon and over ,
The patient ice above and beneath , shall liquidate .

And with an arrogant diligence ,
They will set out on their quest ,
To gain their wealth ,
At the loss of other's health .
The sweat and hard work of the many ,
Will feed and fatten a few elite more and more ,
Until they can not pass through my door .

They shall burn the bones of their kin and brothers ,
Shed their blood , make them suffer .
All the lands they shall exploit from the core ,
Till upon them they can live no more .

In all their rivers they shall dump their flesh and trash ,
Till their waters induce a burning rash .
They'll live to be a 100 no more ,
What the hell would they do if they lived for three or four ?!

Their lives are mere particles of flesh in this universe ,
All so vast in degree .
Their petty lives are but tiny drops ,
In this soaring endless sea of history .

Is it their wish to bury their gold and paper cash ,
Within their grave in a stash ?

Beauty and nature is not their product to loot and rob ,
To preserve and cherish is their job .

What they can not create and grant ,
They have no right to take .
Only one earth there is ,
Humanity is at stake .

Beauty is to be treasured as it is ,
To be embraced , praised , and caressed .
They can not derange it's face ,
It is not theirs to possess .

In the end their body ,
Shall be absorbed within the soil all so deep .

And may transform to fresh green grass ,
To feed the sheep .
And from their meat other's shall eat ,
And the circle itself shall repeat .

Or their body , flesh and bone ,
May grow tall by a rigid stone ,
To form a large lively tree ,
If it bears fruit ,
The travelers thirst it shall suit .
If not their restless heat shall fade ,
Beneath it's soothing shade .

Yet where do you think shall go
Their enraged desperate soul ,
As it can not stay within a body or bowl .

If you pour the sea within a glass ,
The glass shall burst at last .

Within their souls I emplaced all of my honor and trust ,
This is why in peace and love strive they must .

Their soul shall again with me unite ,
Just the elements of pure energy ,
No sound nor sight .
Up here with the untarnished conscience ,
They had at birth ,
Whatever in their lifetime they have done ,
They shall see , feel , and hear , personified .
So intense , so vivid , so abrupt , magnified .

And after they're long gone ,
Upon the earth their actions shall create love or grudge ,
And other's shall judge ,
As always time is the best judge , who am I to judge .

The more acute the love or hate ,
That upon the earth they pour ,
The more their memory against time shall endure .

And the wild beasts and priests ,
Who preach of my heaven and hell ,
With no just moral ground ,
In their teachings no love , nor mercy , nor logic can be found .

Who do they think I am ,
A perverted maniac sham ,
To bake them like a steak in the flames of hell ,
And grow back their skin ,
And burn them again from outside within !

Or to have grotesque blood drooling dragons ,
Eat them night and day ,
And shit them out the other way .
Do they take me for a sadistic fool of devastation
To indulge in the affliction of my own creation ?

If they just for a moment think ,

They can see ,
That the God they are preaching is not me .

How can I convict with content ,
A being that was created with no self-intent .
I am more responsible than them ,
I gave them life without their consent .

And the corrupted tale ,
They advocate about my heavens ,
With flowing streams of honey , milk , and wine ,
Is so idiotically non-divine .
For them to indulge in erotic orgies ,
Again and again all day and night ,
With fruity virgin maidens ,
Who always remain glorious tight ,
Masses of flesh , intertwined within each other .....
In a chaos of drunken disorder ,
Is this there vision of heaven upright ?
This is a disgusting freak fright !
I have never heard of a more disgusting place ,
Well if this is my heaven , I am a true disgrace

Yes , lustful virgins of all sorts and kind ,
Have they truly lost their mind .
Who do they conceive me for ,
A universal pimp ;
To hold a 300 meter diamond cane ,
And to walk with a limp ?

These wicked priests ,
Believe in nothing ,
They are only thinking about their feast .

I don't need their kneeling praise ,
In plead of my forgiveness ,
In the end they'll have to ask it ,
From the human conscience ,
Nothing more , nothing less .

I don't need their ground bending prayer
Five times a day , night after day .
For this I have a million innocent angels ,
Before me in a delightful array .

They don't need to search ,
Any divine law dripping book ,
For my presence to possess
I am in one word : love
Nothing more nothing less ,
They can find me in a helping hand , a tender caress
These holy books are for the human business .

To their dreadful deeds in response ,
They speak of my avenging rage ,
They are either hypocrites or ruthless insane ,
Or they just want to keep them in their golden cage .

Think in a blink ,
I gave you a body ,
And made sure to give you a brain .
Let it set you free ,
Not put you in an ignorant tempting restrain .

Either I created you ,
Or you created me ,
Upon ourselves how can we not have mercy ?

And yet I know that a very few ,
Shall rise to create and innovate ,
With the morning dew .
To ease the burden of mankind ,
My strength within their soul ,
Like a fortress they shall find .

If love and science can embrace ,
There are no limits to time and space .

Technology and the human soul ,
If we can combine ,
Like the sun and stars you can forever shine .
With love and knowledge up to the universe ,
Round and round ,
You can spin
With no sight nor sound ,
Up there , down here , and within .

God emerged from this state of meditation ,
To fulfill the prophecy of his creation .
From the tree top ,
He took Adam's broken rib ,
To gently nib that token rib .
And with that sharp portion ,
He created Eve ,
Breathing ; all of his grace ,
To form her flawless face ,

To shape her precious body and heart .
He used all of his inventive art .
For her breast , he extracted the soil of the mountain peaks .
For her eyes , he used the water of the sea's highest tides.
And between her tender ivory thighs he applied
The elements of the leaves from the erotic jungle depths .

Till at last with his creation he was satisfied .
And at the sight of this mortal delight ,
The angels rejoiced in triumph and joy ,
And without the slightest order ,
They all knelt before her in order .

"Oh , Lord , for this delicate crafty creation ,
It was getting late ,
But now we can see that it was worth the wait ."

And then he placed back Adam's rib ,
Within his chest , so firmly strong
That his heart he could no longer take ,
And it would stay where it belonged .

Then the Lord , placed Eve by Adam's side ,
In the jungle under an apple tree ,
He then awoke Adam ,
For his eternal companion , his true love
He would have to see .

Adam let out a sigh ,
Like a wild jungle cry .
He was bedazzled in love within the first glimpse
In the first taste and touch .
And he yearned to hold her so more and much .

As he explored her features ,
He soon realized the purpose of his journey ,
When he recognized the mountain peaks ,
In the firm shape of her ripe breast .
The winding roads ,
Of his love bound journey .
He saw and felt in her fine curves and twists
And then upon her pink bud lips he laid a burning kiss .
Within her deep tranquil eyes ,
He sensed all of the motion of the sea ,
With all the colors and rays of life so playfully .
And between her burning thighs ,
He was absorbed by the severe engulfing jungle heat .

Afraid that his heart ,
Would again shoot out to depart ,
He reached to touch it with his finger tips ,
And then felt reassured that his ribs ,
Had been reinforced ,
And he knew then
That in the end his love would find it's course .

He knew then that the love for Eve ,
He would have to keep within his chest ,
And with her motions and emotions ,
He would have to keep abreast .

And then to thank the Lord he knelt in praise
His hands in gratitude fully raised :

"Oh , Lord you have taken my breath away ,
You have left me speechless in your beauty ,
Thank you Lord , there is nothing more I can say . "

He observed in bewildering fascination ,
How with a wet touch ,
Her body would throb in sensation .

And soon he would realize how they were lock and key ,
Like the sun upon the mountain snow ,
Like the pearl within the shell and the shell within the sea ,
Like the tree in the jungle and the jungle in the spring .

She was a prowling animal so untamed ,
Who was just learning to play the game .
And he sacrificed his everything and all ,
From outside within ,
Inch for inch ,
Skin for skin

And while quenching each other's intense fires ,
They held each other so tight , with so much desire ,
That their hearts and veins beat as one in perfect rhyme ,
To pace life in the atmosphere , in the space of time .

Their firm embrace shaped a shell ,
Strong and solid in structure , form , and foundation ,
To nourish and flourish a pearl of unknown fascination .

"Now my Lord" , Adam Shouted ,

"I have a fresh new quest ,
To explore her everything and all ,
And put our love to the ultimate test .

For her every grain ,
My body and brain ,
So deeply yearn ,
Words can not define my drive ,
I can only burn .

She is your utter master piece ,
Only with her can I live in peace .
Me ; you created so strong , so rough , so bare ,
But she is something else , she is very rare .
Her mind is full of harmony , so real
Yet so abstract ,
And her dignity is always intact .

Her hands are so tender ,
Yet so strong , unlimited , intense , from within ,
They can help me rise to my feet again .

Her heart is ablaze with kindness ,
And her lust only burns for love in caress ,
If there is no compassion , no spark reaction ,
For her body there is no climax , no satisfaction .

She is so simple ,
Yet shall always be a mystery unsolved ,
Like a butterfly around a flame ,
Around her presence I shall revolve .

Her eyes give me direction ,
Her hands guide me to my destiny ,
Nowhere else I want to be ,
But in her arms till infinity .

She speaks my mind ,
Feels my pain and joy ,
And when we finish words ,
Our bodies again rejoin .

With her kiss and in her arms ,
I melt away without a trace ,
Within her cage I feel so wild and free ,
How can I let go from this eternal embrace ?

No longer shall I wonder , no longer shall I roam ,
Her heavenly body is my last and final home .

Yes , with the beauty of her features forevermore ,
No nature I need to explore .

Her budlike lips are pink roses
From creation's early springs ,
They can really make the angels dance and sing .

Her firm large breast ,
Are like the mountain peaks ,
That for my new high ,
I yearn to conquer ,
I yearn to seek .

And between the dove feathers of her thighs ,
I feel the jungle heat all so deep ,
Like a wild animal it makes me leap .

Oh Lord , how can I explain your love and grace ,
You have forever enlightened my stone-aged face .

Only in your hands can a creation form so bold ,
That all the earth's wonders within it one may behold .
No longer shall I again roam ,
In the jungle , by the sea or mountain side ,
We shall build our sacred home .

I am sure with my passion and scorching lust ,
A pearl of love shall finally evolve ; it must .
For my hunger and drive are so bold ,
Only with her gentle touch ,
May love we behold ."

Now my child go to sleep ,
It's getting late ,
The night is dead tired deep ,
And my age is great .

Grandma , I sighed :
When will I find my Eve ?

Oh my dear , all in good time , you will find
When your childhood you leave behind .

The energy of youth shall take you on your quest ,
To find true love and leave all the rest .

And although the nature and wilderness ,
You may not search for many years ,
In the end it shall only be love
That brings down your joyful tears .

God is within you ,
Throbbing in your veins ,
Burning in your heart .
Keep your faith within ,
And carry on as your have always been .

He is in your heart ,
With his love you should never depart .

Down the road , for your love
You too shall break a rib ;
And learn to honor and care ,

And how to protect your crib .

Upon your journey you shall learn ,
To give a helping hand to a brother ,
And you too with his pains shall suffer .

After all we are one kind ,
Why should unity be so hard to find ?

We all share the same passions and emotions ,
Why should our differences create a hatred potion ?

Upon your quest ,
When all you explore ,
You shall find ,
That nothing is worth killing for .

You shall see them spilling each others blood for power ,
And shall learn how with love your greed to devour .

Oh my son , who I so adore
I hope that upon the stormy sea of life ,
You find a safe peaceful shore .

Now go to sleep ,
For my sake , please no longer think .
Maybe one day we will find the missing link .

Summer 2008 Tehran

ای که آتش تبار خونِ جاری ات
به مثابه ی تمامی فریادها ،
لبالب لبریز ز خاک فرو ریخته است
نگاه ی مدهوش ات به عشقِ زمین
در آتش آفتاب شعله ورشد.
و بانگ زنجیر دران ات را
هر سپیده دم ،
مرغان مهاجر با آوایی پُر خراش ،
خواهند خواند ....

تبِ تردیدِ جان ات ،
تابش نور جهان را ،
بر آب و سنگ زلال خواهد ساخت
و برگ مذابِ تاریخ
به زبانه ی درنگی لرزان ورق خواهد خورد .

دی ۱۳۸۹

"نسیمِ شبانه"

تقدیم به علی صارمی

از درزادرزِ برگها ،
نسیم شبانه می خواند ،
ترانه ی این ویزانه را ....

قلب جهان باز استاد ،
آینه های شکسته در تاخیر سحر ،
به خون آغشته گشت .
و خورشیدِ اندیشه
در چشمه های لجن تپیدن گرفت .

خدا در خشمِ حیرتش ،
آبِ دریا ها را فرو بلعید ،
و سرش در جهل آد می
به کوه اندیشی خمیده گشت .

عمق بیستون از حمقِ وطن لرزید .

خورشید را از دیار ما پنهان می کند .

ای ابله
پوزه بر بند و ،
چشم تر بند
توبره ات محکم تر بند !

مرداد ۸۶ کرج

" شریک شیطان "

باز به فسونی ،
دیگ ِ جوشان به لب ِ د یوانگان را
بر هم می زنی ؟!
دیگر این بار
جنون ِ ابله هان ات سپر نمی شود !

بلند گوی های چرند باف ِ مغز کوب ات
شب و روز ،
شهر را توپ باران می کند .

ز وق وق ِ جان خراش لشگر میمون های ات
به کدامین شیر ِ پیری پناه برم ؟!
یکی را بین بر پشت ِ من ،
دیگری در کنارم می دود
آن دیگر لای پای ام می جود !

بلند گوهای نکبت فسون ات
شهر را مرگ باران می کند .

بوی عزا
بر نسیم ِ ابریشمین ِ سپیده دم می وزد ،
و توفان های تاب توی

دیگر لب به جادوی نفرینی و نفرتی ببسته ام !

درمانده و درد مند م
ای بانوی بالا بلند م
به توفانها غرشی کن
و زار بر بادهای مرگزای تهی بخند ....

کوچ ِ این قبیله ی برد گی را
به افقهای باز کاروان سالاری باش
کاروان سالاری باش ....

ای که از تبار ِ خون ِ آتشینی
این خاک ِ اسیر
به زنجیر ِ جهل و جنون را شهریاری باش
شهریاری باش ....

خرداد ۸۶ تهران

"شهریار"
تقدیم به تمامی بانوان ایران زمین

با آغوش نرم خویش
نسیم آزادی را پناهی باش

با نفس گرم خویش
دل سوخته ام را آتشین آهی باش

با چشمان پر شرم خویش
مرا بدان جاودان واحه روشن راهی باش

در این شب چرکین هزار توی
که بوی لجن ز سیاهی آن جاری ست
خدا یا ، دیگر بس است ،
جان میدهم برای ذره ای ز نورت ،
عاشقان پلک ناخسته را فرجام خونین پگاهی باش

x x x x x x

خسته و جان گسسته ام ،
ای بانوی سینه فراخ من
بیا در آغوشم گیر تا در هم آب شویم
پس ره خورشید کجاست ؟
ای همسفر کوه و سنگلاخ من

گویدم :

" هین و هینت خموش کوبم بر سرت شوی سخت مدهوش

به گمانت ز خویش پریشی ات اشکی غلتد ز چشمِ پلنگانِ یوزِ من ؟

با این جانِ آشفته ای که تو داری ، سر به شرق یا که غرب میسپاری ؟!

تن به رزم می گماری ؟! بر بادت می دهد حتی اندک گوزِ من ! "

گویمش :

" با این حیوان رخساری که تو داری سَزد که سر کنی به اندر غاری ، شب تا

روز دست به دعا بر آری که چون خونفرش گسترانی ز بغداد تا قُندوز من !

پگاه تا بیگاه نام خدا بر زبان رانید ، دست به اندر خشتک کلام الله می خوانید ،

وآنگاه زر در کیسه ی خود می چپانید ، با شمایم ای رهبرانِ پفیوزِ من !

همه اشعارم برای یک کلام ، همه دفترم فدای یک نام ، مرگِ آهنینم ده

زین زندگی رنگینم به ، تمام ، جمله روزگارانم به فدای یک آزاد روزِ من !! "

تابستان ۸۷ - کرج

"یک روز، آزاد "

دریغا عشق بلند خورشید و لرزان پیسوز من

وان رقصِ پیچاپیچِ تو و چشمانِ دریوز من

دریغا کوه و کمرِ جاده های تنت ، و دستانِ خسته ی من

دریغا خطوطِ لبانِ تب زده ی تو و بوسه های لب دوز من

دست در دست ، در کوچه ی خاطراتم با من قدم مزن ،

بر زمینت میکشاند این گوژ پشت و خمیده قوز من

چند در جنگِ عشقِ من بر آیی و چنگ بر سینه ام زنی ؟

هشدار و عقبگرد کن که میسوزاندت این اشکِ جهان افروز من

خدایا بر مغزم گشودی گنجینه ی رازهای گیتی را ، و درِ آن

ببستی زود ، مگر هم به دست توست کلیدِ صندوقِ سینه ی رموز من ؟

خمش ، شب را بی چراغ و بی شراب تاب آورده ای ، سنگ را

به رود بسپار ، چه دانی که چون شود فردای روز من ؟

xxxxxx

بوزینه پوزه ای ، انچوچکی گویی حلقه ی مفقودی "داروین"

به دستی چماقی و به دستی دیگر دیوان اشعار چلغوز من

"روایت"

آن نگاه آن نوازش که جنون مي طلبد
آن سر افراز عشق آن ستايش که خون مي طلبد

آن تپش چون صلا آن اشتياق آن تمناي بي ريا
آن چشمان چون صحرا که گشت و گذار مجنون مي طلبد

از عشق اندک بگوي زندگي را در دل بجوي
فراق را ديگر مپوي که برهوت و هامون مي طلبد

تن هشتن و جان کشتن به گاه بي سخاوتي خاک
بي باک بربارهاي آزنوشتن که : آن پاک شمارا واژگون مي طلبد

گم کرده ايم ره، خانه را، اصل بر ظاهر، ديوانه را
وين دل بيگانه را، وه که نمي باده و کفي افيون مي طلبد

هاي خموش، نگويم ديگربارت : غزل و افسانه مخوان،
ديو را زخانه بران، هرچند کين پيکارت افسون مي طلبد

زمستان ٧٦ تهران

بر مي خيزم به دياري روشن
با نفسهايت پاك
با زمزمه ات مژده سپيده دم
بر مي خيزم تا در سيمآب سحرگاه بشويم تن .

تابستان ۷۵ تهران

"دياري روشن"

برمي خيزم به دياري روشن
با نفسهايت پاك
با زمزمه ات مژده سپيده دم
برمي خيزم تا در سيمآ ب سحرگاه بشويم تن

نرم نرمك بوسه اي و
نوازشي آرام آرام
ملرز نازنينم
عشق هنوز زنده ست
به زير اين ترك خورده بام

در قلبم دارم من
شعر شبانه را
بر مي خيزم به نبرد دروغ و تيرگي
مهر و لطافت توست مرا جوشن

و بر خواهيم خاست بي باك چون پاك
وخواهيم زيست افسانه را
وگل خواهيم كاشت در ميان آهن
به ياد داري شعر شبانه را ؟!

"رقصِ با شیران"

رقصِ با شیرانت چه شد ، بانگِ فتحِ د لیرانت کجاست ؟
شیدِ رهنمای انیرانت چه شد ، پندِ پیرانت کجاست ؟

بر این توربتِ پاکِ جمشیدِ جم آهسته نه قدم
حرمتِ خاکِ آرامگه سالارِ امیرانت کجاست ؟

جان بردر تب و بغض بر لبِ زین حاکمانِ بیگانه ، با این
نشانهای غریبانه، شاهنشاه ی فرزانه و شیر و خورشیدِ ایرانت کجاست ؟

واژه ها میگردد به دورِ سرم ، د شمن یا د شمنام تا کدام آید به برم
کلامِ عشق را ز لبت کی ربود ؟ غزلِ د لپذ یرانت کجاست ؟

پگاه تا بیگاه قهقهه ی اهریمن طنین انداز است در شهرِ ما ، خدا یا
رحمی بدین دهرِ ما ، قلبِ دیو شکاف گیو تیرانت کجاست ؟

ابلیس اژدهای هفت سر شده ست بر ملکِ ما سایه گستر
تیغِ کدامین مرد سینه او شکافد ، رستمِ تیزِ شمشیرانت کجاست ؟

ای ایران ! گلهای مهربانی فسرد ند ، خاطره های عاشقانه همه مرد ند
یارانت به پیشِ دوستاقبانانشان جان سپردند ، جنبش و جهد اسیرانت کجاست ؟
بهار ٨٦ تهران

"درد یاران"

برای دکترعلی رضا نوری زاده

خدا خنده ای بر لبانت نهد ای مرد!
با این باری که تو داری
وآهسته و صبور ، عرق ریزان
آنرا بر دوش به سوی سر منزلِ آئینه ها می بری
خدا دستانِ گشاده تری به تو دهد ای مرد
کینچنین بی دریغ و جانفشان دردِ یارانِ دربند را
از سینه به سینه ها می بری

خرداد ۸۵ تهران

"باغ عدن"

جرقه های آتشین ِ در شب فضای ِ کهکشانهای ِ جاودانه
حاصل ِ دو انفجار ِ روی در روی ز هم آغوشی ی عاشقانه !
xx xx xx xx

بزن نم نم بزن نوک نوک در دهانم طعام ِ عشق ره آورد
پرواز ِ پر فرسا را ، چونکه فرود آمدی در آشیانه

بزن کم کم بزن دم دم بزن بر هم بزدای همه
آلودگی ها ز تن و جانم با توک بوسه های جانانه

سر به شانه ات می نهم و در آغوشت جان می دهم
سحر با بوسه ای به رستاخیزی دیگر چشم میگشایم مستانه

آن بوسه های غنچه سایت دیری ست چه فروزان در دهانم
شکفته است گل ِ عشق را ، کجاست سر گشته شمع جوی پروانه ؟

وآن لبهای پیاله پیمایت مرا به چنان گیج اندر گیج جنونی سر مست
کرده است ، دیگر نمیدانم این منم یا تویی که پی در پی میپیماید پیمانه

شرر سان باده ای نوشیده ام که تا ابد عربده کشان خواهم بود ، ندهم جرعه ای
به کس، مستی زین دست شیشه به دست دیده اید که فُوق کند میخانه ؟

عشق ما در امتداد هستی جهان را چه خوش آراسته است : باغ عدنم
این خانه و پستانهایت سیب بهشتی و هیچ جبار خدایی نیست در میانه !
خرداد ۸۶ - کرج

"زنجیرِ طلایی ات مبارک"

به گاه ی اوجِ شادی ،
رها در عشقبازیِ فیلسوفانه ی بهاری ،
و سرِ کله ی نوزادی –
عطر افشانِ آزادی .....

×××

نه دشنه ،
نه قلم ،
اندر آید به کف

با دستهای ورم کرده ،
خاک را چون باید کا فت ؟!

دیگر امسال ،
دستانِ خسته ی مفصل بشکسته ای ،
زنجیرِ پاهای ات را ،
از طلا ،
خواهند با فت :
مبارک بادات !

فروردین ۸۷ - کرج

بیا با هم
نرم نرمک بگرییم
بازمانده قطره‌های عشق را
که نیست دیگر نشانی ز تازه گي و پاکیزه گي

درین درنده دشت بي صفت
با نگاه و نوازش و عریاني خویش
دعوتم کن به ضیافتِ عصمت و دوشیزه گي

مي دانم
دیگر نه چراغ است و نه راه
نه حتي تک درختي ما را سر پناه
نه زمزمه ی خشک جویی
نه ناله اي نه فریادي ز سویی
دیگر دیري ست که مرد
هر چه عاشقانه ست در دیار ما

نگاه را
به وراي این د شتِ ظلمت گستر باید برد
....باید برد

تابستان – ۱۳۷۴ تهران

"هجرت"

خنكاي گيسوانت را بر چهره ی من رها کن
مي خواهم شبنم كوهي دوردست ترين آبشاران بنوشم

نمي بيني لبم خشك و تنم تب زده
نيافتم قطره نشاني زان سر چشمه ازلي
درين صحراي شب زده

بوسه هاي عطر آگين نثار مرا كن
مي خواهم شيره ي گلهاي نخستين بهاران را بنوشم

نان مارا در لجنزاران نهاده اند
واي چه دردي ست
عاشقانه ها را با دستهاي چركين سرودن
ز رنج و اشك انسان
تا سحر نغنودن
اما مطرود همگنان بودن
واي چه درد سردي ست

چگويم پلاسم خود گوياي همه پير و پوده حقيقت هاست
چه غبار آلود و شوخگين و حيران که منم
نيافتم نچشيدم جرعه اي زان جاودان زلال
چكنم گرم شرم نايد ز چشمه ي پاك سخنم

ز نواله ی گلو گیرا ت بنا ل ....

تو ای مادر ،

به گمانم

بر آوردی پیچ فریادی بلند

ز جان ات همه درد مند   :

" خدا یا ،

دیگر نخواهم بخشود ترا " !!

مرداد ۸۷ - کرج

سال

به

سا ل ......

بنشد دیگر گون هیچ ،

تنها فزون گشته

چروک پوست چرم سای ات

پینه اندر پیچ ،

بنشد دیگر گون ،

هیچ !

نگاه ات گویای غم قرون است

که به نبرد های زمانی دور می بردم

و بازوان ات چقدر از نفرت سترون است

با آنکه جنازه ی کشتگان ات را

هماره به دوش کشیده ای !

از گذشته تا به حال ،

واي اما ، اگرت زينسان مي بايد بودن

که به زير اژدها

تو خود آن گنج نهفته بودي

× × ×

قيام گويان

اي خدا جويان ِ حرم خانه نشين

بنگريد چنين بي دين و بي دنيا دل كنده اي

ای سجود ِ پر جود و سرد ت

بر ناله و نفرت ما

طرح تلخ خنده ای

"خرسند"

تقديم به مادر زن از جان گذ شته ام : خرسند

از گذشته

تا

به حا ل ....

آه تو خود گفته بودي...

بسي بيابان و كوه و كمر
به عشق ِ آن جاويد هستي
بسي فراز و پستي
پيموده ام
واي از آن شب سرشتنهايت
كه ام رنج دانه اي ست ، چنان پاك
نبخشم به هر گونه خاك
واي از آن كشتنهايت

بسا شب كه بي چراغ سحر كردم
بسا نان كه در خون ِ جگر تر كردم

ز گلويم به پيش ِ گزمكان
غم و غرور ِ اياران را فرو بردم
گر اينچنينش بالا آوردم:

هاي مرد با توام من ديوانه شده ام
ز خويش ريش و ز كيش
حسرتي و نفرتي نماندستم بيش
بي خدا و بي شرمم خواندند
به تيپاي ز خانه ام راندند
زدند بسي سنگ بر سرم
گر اينچنين مست به در ِ ميخانه شده ام

آي مگوي مي دانم
تو خود گفته بودي

"مرثیه"

برای زنده یا د:
مهدی اخوان ثالث ، که از او دریغ کلامی
نتوانم گفت

اي كلامت تلختر ز زهري
كه در جام نبرد مردان فتاد
راز سوخته دلان را
كي اينچنين گرم با تو در ميان نهاد
كه ما را ز سوز آن همه در آتش فكنده اي ؟
اي وجود پر جود و دردت
بر حيرت و حيراني ما طرح تلخ خنده اي

× × ×

تو خود گفته بودي
جايي در آن فراسوهاست
كه پيران عشق سوخته
به بخشش افيون شعر و جام مهر
به ما مجنونان ه تشنه و چشم دوخته
گرد هم آيند.
ومارا زخلوص آن پايكوبي و هاي هوهاست
و پروانگان دلجوي و غنچه هاي بكر گوي
اين عشاق باغ را آذين غوغاست
و رقص دوشيزگان آتش و باد
چنان است كه گويي دشمني نيست باد

"در سوگ بامداد"

برای زنده یاد جاودان استاد : احمد شاملو

بغض ِ سپیده شکفت
بالهاي بانگي ست
،افق پیماي
ز نهفت

نازنینا!
مي داني دیگر چه هنگامي ست ؟
سوگ ِ کدامین عا شق ِ گمنامي ست ؟

چشمان مرا جگربار می خواهند

فروردین ۸۷ کرج

"باژگونه تر"

خوشترین روزگارم ،
در قابی شکسته ،
نهان است

تلخترین ساعاتم ،
بر امواج ِ رقص ِ جادویی ات ،
روان است

دهانم ز سخن بی نیاز بود
و دلم ز بوسه ،
به هنگامی که با چشمانت ،
د نیا را ،
باژگونه تر ،
به روی ام دواندی

نفرین بدین بغض و ،
نفرین به آفریننده ی آن
نفرین بدین دستان
که تنها جاجیم ِ فاصله می بافند

نفرین بدان چشمانی که

"لبریز"

بوی باران و باروت

از دهانِ شب جاری ست .

آسمان در اخمِ مهیب اش فسرده ست

و نورِ نفرینی ستارگان ،

بر جبین ات می درخشد .

پای ات بر خاکسترِ تفتِ خاک و

حسرتِ عشقی نمور

که گلوی ات را فشرده ست .

بهمن ۸۷ کرج

" عاشقانه : سحر گاهانه "

باز برای شهلا همیشه

شهامتِ خنده های بیداری و ،
نوازشهای بی قراری
سلامی از جنسِ خورشید و ،
اشکی از جنسِ سحر
بوسه های کهکشانی و ،
عطرِ تنی آسمانی

باری ،

نازنینم ،

دیگر چه می خواهم ؟

دیگر چه توانی ؟

دی ۸۶ نوشهر

"افکار طلایی"

برکتخانه‌ی بی بهای ات
رنگِ کثافت گرفته ست .
ای که برای چنگ نوازیِ درخششِ مدفوع اربابان ات
در تکاپو خود را هلاک کرده ای ....

های های و هیاهو
صدای بوق و دودِ سحرگاهان
کرمخون خسته را
در رگهای ات می تپاند

تناسبِ اندام ات
به هم ریخته ست
رو به روی آینه در آی
و جامه بر کن
خشتک را سرت کش

رحمی به ما کن
لبریز بوی ات
از دماغِ ما بیرون زده ست !
آذر ۸۶ کرج

" بار "

رقیباند فراوان ،

شاخ ات را ،

خوب تیز گردان !

زین ات را ،

نیک برق بیانداز

شاید فردا ،

از فراز ،

شهنشاهی ،

نصیب تو شود باز !

دی ۸۶ - تهران

" چرک سروده "

گفتی :
" با این قلبِ پرخونِ لجنی که تو داری
بار اندازیِ کلان باید ات "
ده جفت چکمه ی چرمین پوساندم در این راه و... : آه ....

گفتی :
" ای رفیق ،
با این دردی که تو داری
ده کوزه می گدازان باید ات "
بیستمی را هم سر کشیدم و اثر نکرد

بر مخم گوزیدند و ،
قلبم را دریدند ،
وباز از من ترانه و شعر طلب دارند ؟!

روی به روی آینه هر روز برای خودم
دوازده شکلکِ روزانه در می آورم
ودلم را به جفنگهای این چرتکِ قلم خوش کردم ....

به مدفوعم خیره می نگرم
همانگونه که به دفتر چرک سروده های ام
چکنم که دلنشینترین افکارم
در مستراح از گذرگاه ی خاطرم عبور می کند
بهمن ۸۶ تهران

"عقوبت"

هزار پدرت

برلاشه ی زخاک پس زده ات

نخواهند گریست

ای که بوی گند ا ت

جهنم را نیز آشفته می کند!

شکوفه ها سربریدی و

عصمت ِ ستارگان دریدی ؟!

باش تا آفتاب

پوست ِ چربت را

برای ضیا فت ِ کرکسان بتفتاند

می شنوی ؟

این ناله ی نوحه گران

در پس ِ پشت ِ جنازه ی باد کرده ات نیست...

غوغای شهوتناک ِ هجوم ِ لاشخواران ا ست

تف کرده و پوزه هایشان کف کرده و

سرشار و مست

ز بوی پخته ی تن ِ فربه ات

و هزار هرزه پدرت

به پیش ِ دریده چشمت

یکجا

مادرت را...

تقسیم خواهند کرد!

تیر ۸۶ کرج

"برآمدن"

و باز برای شهلا البته

عمرم را می شنوم ،
که از روی عقربه ی ثانیه شمار می چکد ،
ودر سکوتِ ساکنِ شب ،
با آوایی تهی ،
گام می زند .

نامم چون کبکِ زده واژگانم می شکند
و کهنه دفترِ اشعارم ،
زندانِ منست .

ای که رگانت سرنوشتِ مرا هدایت می کند
و دستانت از درد می گوید
نگاه ات
مفهومِ جاذ به ست ....
مرا بکشان
که تا فرود آیم ،
بر زمینِ ناهموار
بنشینم
و زار ،
بر خویشتن ،
به سرود آیم .
شهریور ۸۶ - کرج

ذبحِ قربانی ،
تقدیم به خداوندانت !

دی ۸۶ - تهران

«ذبح»

تقدیم به بانوی بی نظیر بوتو
که قتل او قلبم را سخت شکست

بسوز و بسوزان
در آتش ِ خویشتن ،
با آن خونچکان دانش ِ پیامبرانت
همه شیدای آرزو های پست

بسوز و بسوزان ،
هر چه بود و شد و هست
بسوزان
هر چه رست !

ای خفته در فراسوی مرزهای تاریخ ،
چشم فرو بند
بر خونفریاد ِ فرزندانت

مخمور بیآرام ،
در تابوتِ معبدِ نفرتخوانت

بسوز و بسوزان ،
اینچنین و آنچندانت !

بانوی زیبا روی اشراق ،

و نمی دانی چرا بسی زود تر یا اندکی دیر تر
چشم بنگشودی ،
در پسین یا پشینِ گیجِ جهان ...

آه ، این جهان ....
آه ، این جهان را ....

حیرتا ،
ناله و نفرینِ زمین و زمان را ،
نمی شنوی ؟!

ز غژغژ تضادِ دو گوز پیچِ گیجِ جهان ات ،
دهان به انگشت ،

نمی شوی ؟!

دی ۸۶ - کرج

"گیج جهان"

مهتاب :
نفرینِ نوریِ چرکتاب

خورشید :
سرخندِ کنایتی از امید

باد :
قاصدِ فریادهای رفته از یاد

باران :
زار گریه های شورِ خداوندگاران

آزادی :
فریبی طنز آلود

عشق :
حسرتی کبود

ارزشِ انسان ، به کیلو
حراجِ خدا ، به یورو

و توئی انسانِ خویشْ پالا
که سر پا نشناس ایستاده ای
بر مرکز این گوزْ پیچِ جهان
وز این همه لبریزی ....

"نوازشهاي اهورایی"

براي دخترکم : پگاه

اي که نگاه ي معصومت
عريان بر صليب ِ گناهانم مي کوبد
اي بازتاب ِ بازمانده باورهاي باآوريهايم
اشکت گويي شبنمي ست روشن
تک ستاره ي کوير ِ در به در يهايم
که مي تراود بر لبان ِ برآماسيده ام
تا ديگرباره به جستجوي سرمنزل ِ آيينه ها بر خيزم
بازوان ِ کوچکت جانپناه ي اين تن ِ رنج کشيده ام
پايان ِ شبنامه ي بي ياوريهايم

نخستين لبخند ِ پگاهت
واپسين آه ي من بود
چرا که دانستم
ماندني ترين آفريده ي عشق ِ خداوندي
از روحي فرشته وار
در تو دميدن گرفته ست

و ابليس ِ خانه
با نوازهاي اهورايي ات
آرميدن گرفته ست
پاييز ۱۳۷۸ زندان اوين - تهران

روسپي زادگان حكمران و كامجويان،

ز گندآب و غوغاي و سودايش.

خداي را

دريغا مردي ! مددي

مهلتِ انديشه اي،

ريشه ژرف د ر خون است

مولاي را،

دريغا تيشه اي!

xxxxx

چنان چون

زمزمه هاي داناتر پيري

به چاه اند رون

زندگي بمن آموخته ست خاموشي را

يا .... بله .....فراموشي را.....

تابستان ۷۸ زندان اوين

"زمزمه اي د ر سوگ وطن"

چنان چون زمزمه هاي داناتر پيري به چاه اندرون
زندگي به من آموخته ست
خاموشي را.

xxxx

آه اي نسلِ بي شرم و گريزان ز آيينه ها
نفرت انگيزد آيين بودت .
حيرتم زجاي دندانِ دستِ نان باخته ست و،
چهره هاي اين انسان وشان
نيست هيچمان اشكي آزرمي بدين وجودت ؟

نمي دانم باد نفسِ كدام اهريمني تر،
چنين كولاك فصلي فراموشي گستر
به ديارِ ما آورده ست

فصلِ بيداد
فصلِ شگرفترتضاد
سالار سردا ر سواري نمي آيد ز قعله به در
نيست چراغِ بيدار دلي،
زمزمه اي، نويد يي،
ز اهلِ دلي،
نيست يكدم پرتوي گرمي ،الها مي ، ز خورشيد

،شهر ماست،
با دوده ي خواب آور فضايش.

"وسوسه"

تو مانده ای و ،

وسوسه ی کشنده ی مرگ

تا شیطان ات ،

در نی لبکی دمد

و دو روحِ دود وار ز جسم ات ،

به رقصی جادویی برخیزند .

از تن ات خواهند کند ،

تاوانِ نشیبی دراز

وین فرودِ بی فراز

از پیش بر پیشانی ام بوسه زن و ،

مرگم را بستا

که خدای من هماره

در نوازشهای تو جاری ست .

مهر ۸۷ - کرج

لبریزِ کیف می شوید

دیگر به سوی شما باز نخواهم گشت

ای که مادرانِ اتان را تشنه لب

به زنجیر

به دور میدانِ گیجِ پیچِ تابستان

چوبِ حراج می زنید

دیگر به سوی شما باز نخواهم گشت
ای که پیرانِ اتان را
پشاپیش

گودال و گور می کنید

دیگر به سوی شما باز نخواهم گشت

تابستان ۸۷ - تهران

"باز نخواهم گشت"

نفرین وار

بارهای بار

به سوی شهرتان ُ تف ِ غلیظ ِ د شنام فرستادم و ،

باز به ناچار

به سوی هوای اسیدگون ِ آن ،

که مانند ِ دیوارهای آهنین ،

زنگزده ،

بلند ،

از هیچ حفاظت می کنند ،

باز گشتم
ای پرورد گار ِ مغموم

چه حاصلی ست

زین آفرینش ِ موهوم ؟
× × ×
ای که ز بوی سرشار ِ خشتک ِ زنهای اتان

مبدل در تصوری مُدور ،

برپا شده ،

فرجام می گیرد و ،

تکرار می پذیرد ...

وین وسوسه ی هرگز و همیشه را ،

پایانی نیست ....

زمستان ۸۷ - کرج

جای جلیسِ خدا با شیطان

باژگونه شد ...

ای شیخِ نخل و واحه‌ی ما ،

در دستت خشتکِ زنهای‌ات چون درفشی و ،

بر چهره‌ات آن خون چکان کتابت چون نقابت !

کاش بودی و می‌دیدی

که چگونه عصا به دستان را به رقابت انداخته است ،

حدیثِ شیر و شرابت ....

و برشِ زهرآگینِ شمشیرِ خود را ،

برنیمه‌ی پیکرِ مُدورِ زمان

با چشمانِ خود می‌چشیدی !

ای ابله‌ی دورانها ،

هیچ چیز حتی جان‌ات تا ابد آرام نمی‌گیرد

که در امتدادِ زمان رشته رشته ،

گسسته و ،

باز به هم پیوسته ،

"شیخ نخل و واحه ....تکرار "

تاب آ تاب

پیچ آ پیچ

بالای سر پوچ ِ پوچ و ،

به پیش پای ات هیچ ِ هیچ .

کیش آ کیش

ریش آ ریش

پس آ پس و ،

پیش آ پیش

تصویرِ شکسته و پریشی ...

خطورِ وسوسه ی کشنده ی عشق و انسان

د ر خاطری هلاک اندیش ....

در چرخشی مهیب و رُمبان

در لحظه ای و هزاره ای

زمین با آسمان

"در چشمان هر غریبه ای "

بر توفانها بال گشوده ام من

با حیرت ِ اوجی و بر باد موجی و،

فرودی گیج سخت

ز روز ِ نخست بد ین سان بوده ام من

همان باخته پاکی که بر سر ِ هر گذر بینی

با چنگ ِ طلب بر گریبان ِ بخت

بیت ِ آخر ز اول سروده ام من

و به هنگامی که به جستجوی مادر ِ خویش

کوچه اندر کوچه پیمود...

نامم را بر سر زبان ِ هر هرزه ای شنوده ام من

و خود را در چشمان ِ هر غریبه ای یافتم.

تهران تابستان ۸۷

خواهم اتان د يد

با التماس و پوزشی

که پوزه های پیر اتان را جنبانده ست !!

تیر ما ۸۶- تهران

دیگر صبر و توانِ بیانِ احساسم نیست !

یا خوانم ده

یا تخم ات می کنم

دیگر جایی بر این کهنه پلاسم نیست !

چند زنی

با تازیانه ی خون چکان ات

بر پیکرِ کفیده ام ؟

بترس کین خرِ زر کش نیز خدایی دارد !

بشنو و در هراس غوطه ور شو

عرعرم چار ستونِ کاخهای اتان رمبانده ست

روزی تا گردن فرو

دست پا زنان

در باتلاقِ مد فوع ام

"سه سرود برای حیوانات اهلی ، وحشی ، و میانه رو"

در گه ی خویش غلتید ن ات ،

ای حیوان ،

زین سان چرید ن ات

گویاست شعورت !

ارباب ات با شلاق آمده

برای آرمید ن ات ،

ای حیوان ،

پوز فرو بند و بخسپ

در چشم ِ عالم کورت

_____

یا نانم ده

یا شکم ات می درم

" از راه "

چشمانم :
الماس ستارگانی
که ز گنجینه ی سلیمان ربوده شد
تا کسوفِ مسیح را
،درخششی باشند،
و شاهدانی بر سقوطِ بیت المقدس،
ترک های چرکچکانِ پوستینِ خشکید ه ام :
رگه های مارگونه ی صحرای عربستان .

زبانم :
راهی ست بر جاده ی ابریشم
که از دربارِ کاخِ هارون
تا زیرزمینهای زندان اوین امتداد دارد .

و دستانم :
دو برگِ زیتونِ لرزان ،
که ز رگهایم
که با قلبِ فرات می تپند
تغذیه می کنند

آبان ۱۳۸۹ کرج

فضا ،

فضای کوبش ِ کوسها ،

به خوانش ِ سپه سالاری ست

زمان ،

زمان ِ آویختن ِ هر دینْ دکانداری ،

بر سر هر سپیداری ست !

فروردین ۸۷ - کرج

"پچپچه ی زنجیر ها"

میان بودن و شدن ،
زمان و فضا بی انتها ست ،
در آن شناور شو

این پژواکِ پچپچه های پیچانِ زنجیر هاست ،
که کوچه ها را ،
تا دندان ،
به لرزه آورده ست ،
بشنو :

"آه کشید !
ای از خویش بیگانگان ، آه کشید !
از اعماقِ جان ،
ای گرسنگان ،
درماندگان ،
زنجیریان ،

دیوانگان ، آه کشید !

تا طوفانِ آتشی ،
شعله ور کنید ،
در میانِ صنوبر های رقصان ، آه کشید ! "

" تاراج "

خدا یا ،
چه دانستم
که گل در ریشه هایش اسیر شود
بر حقلِ آن فرو پیچیده
بر گردِ نش زنجیر شود

×××

نمی دانی ،
غروبِ چشمانت
در سایه ی ابرِ مژگانِ جگر بارت
چه غمی دارد مهربانم !

بر مزارِ پدرانت زار ،
انفجارِ بغضِ هزار و چهار صد ساله ات را ،
نگریستم

و آنگاه بر خود ،
چو دریای مازندرانم .... ،
عاشقانه گریستم !

آبان ۸۶ - کرج

" آه و عطش : وطنم "

ای آفتابِ نیم رمقِ آرزوهای ام

بدرخش ،

با این اشکِ ،

لحظه ای

بر پیکرِ سردِ وطن

چه کلامی

چه کتابی

تفسیر گرِ این اشکِ ؟

چه آهی

چه آبی

سیرابِ این عطش

فروکش این آتش ؟

بهمن ۸۶ - کرج

"تپش"

تپش ِ طبل ِ سای قلب ات ،
آیینه ها را فرو ریخته است
تا در تاریکی ،
رطوبت ِ خطوط ِ چهره ات را
با سرانگشتانم
ترسیم کنم

شکست ها و گذ شت ها
ترا در من فرو برده است
عریانی ات ،
تن
می لرزاندم

و آه انتظار
در واپسین نفس

تا در جاودانی ات
جاری شوم

بهمن ۸۶ - تهران

به کیسه آردی فروختند
به اشکِ زردی
که برای طلا فرو غلتید
به حسرتخندی
که از کنارِ گوشت گذشت ....

و به رهبرانِ حیوان رخساری
که سزَد ماوای اشان به اند ر غاری
که هرگز نمی به چشم ندارند و ،
سخت بر گُرده ی جهان
به نماز ایستاده اند
و دیری ست اندیشه و احساس را وداع گفتند

آیا به راستی
فرمانِ این آتش آشوب را ،
خدای آنها داده است ؟!؟!

تیر ۸۷ تهران

"معما"

ابری سیاه ،

ساکت و ،

سنگین

بر دیارِ ما ،

هیبت افکنده است ....

انفجارهای مغز جنبان

به قیمتِ نانِ فرزندانِ بغداد

چرکمرده خونفرشی گسترده

از بصره تا کابل ....

شمشیر و مسلسل

صفِ دلقکانِ بیروت را

به آشوب کشانده ست

و گردبادِ گنگِ تابِ سوزانِ سام

ریشِ عمو سام را

پریشانده ست ....

این معما را

در صحنِ کدامین پیرِ نجف

قرایت کنم ؟

ستاره های بخت را

به پیش کدامین رمالِ دنیا دوره گردی

فرو ریزم ؟

به سالی که دخترانِ قبیله را

"شیطان و خاکستر"

شیطان و خاکستر ،
لب به لب ،
سر به سر ....

عقل با ابلیس و ،
دل ،
با خدا

اندیشه در بند آزادی و ،
لب ،
در ناسزا

خاکستر و شیطان ،
کابل،
به بغداد و ،
از بغداد ......
به پاسارگاد !

تابستان ۸۷ - تهران

چنین است گر زینسان می کنم های های
می گسلد آخر این سینه می دانم وای

آه انگار که دیگر نیستم
همچو جانی که در پیچ و خم تکاپوها
اندک اندک محو می شود
دیگر ندانم کی رفتم کی ماندم
عاشقانه تر سرودی خواندم

تابستان ۷۹ - مشهد

"عاشقانه تر"

زلالِ چشمانت زجوشش کدامین چشمه ست
کینچنین می شویدم پاک
تا بجلوه ی خویش پی برم
...زعشقِ آفرینش بوسه نهم بر خاک

صداقتِ دستانت بي رحم است و تشنه نواز
رشک و اشک هر مجنون بيابان ديده اي
و دو فانوس اشکت شبتا بهايي که مي نمايند م
داغِ لاله هاي باغِ محبت را راز

،از تاريکترين اقصا
،از دورترين آفاق
مي دهم ره آورد ت همه مهرباني ها را
به گيسوانت وحشي ترين شقايق ها را مي آويزم
تا ريش خويشان ز ياد بري
.روزگار پريشاني ها را

فان پاره اي ، بوسه اي و
وعده ی ديداري بس
اندوه ی عشقي و شوق تني
نوازشي و اندوهگسا ري بس

جواني نيست
تبي نيست
هذيان نيمه شبي نيست
ديرينه عشقي ست
د ر سينه ی کوه
که د ر من تپيدن گرفته ست

"خاطره"

نطفه ی بایسته ات

جاری ،

در جسم ِ خاک ...

می مانی ،

یا

می روی ...

نمی بینی ،

ولی

می شنوی

صوتی نورسا

به غریو می کشاند ات

و مانوس تصویری دور د ست

در خاطر می ماند ات

بهمن ۸۶ - تهران

" آفرینش "

جوشش ِ اندیشه ای ،
فوران ِ احساسی و ،

نوسان ِ حالتی
اشکی ،

لبخنده ای و ،

رعشه ی دستی

و آنگاهت ،

به پدید آمدی ....

دی ۸۶ - تهران

فرمانِ خدای ات را ،
در بوسه ای و نوازشی خلاصه می کنم ...
ناله ، رفت
نواله ، رفت
بغداد و بنگاله رفت
تا گند تقدیسِ خود را
در آبهای ملال "گنگ"
شستیم ، تاروپود
در کنارِ معبدی
که شعله های آنرا
دستِ پدرانمان هزاره ای پیش
بر افروخته بود ...

و آبهای پر ملال
بر آتش
به سوگی جاودانه نشسته ست ....

آبان ۸۶ - کرج

"آبهای پرملال"
تمامی صخره های زندگانی را
برای گوشه ای رهایی ، در نوردیدم
تا که در مشبکِ التماسِ نگاهت ،
عریان ،
گرویدم ...

عمر رفت
مال رفت
حال رفت
تا برهنه در نظاره هم ایستاد یم

مرگ رفت
برگ رفت
توفان و تگرگ رفت
و در آن دم که توان در توشه ی ما ذره ای بود
سر افراز به خاک اوفتاد یم ...

گر که عشقی هست
جنگی هست !
گر که سنگی هست
درنگی هست !
گر که مُلای بی حیایی هست
تفنگی هست !
دست و پا زد نت
مرا به اندیشه فرو برده ست
و گستره ی آرزوهای ات را ،
فریاد ها و کوبشِ بازوهای ات را ،

× × ×

در سرت غوغای بازی چوگان است

خموش ای ابله !

خموش ای پسرک ِ ٤٠ ساله ی کوچولوی ....

تمامی منطق ات هنوز اندر همین واژگان است :

ای دا دا ای دو دو ای دو دو ی.....

و باز از این سوی بدان سوی .....

اسفند ٨٧ - تهران

که با واژگانت بازی می کنی ،

از این سوی بدان سوی

اکنون تمامی جاننوشته های ات را

بر کفِ ترازویی نه ،

تا به وزنِ آن

کسی شاید نانی به تو بخشد !

تو چون رودی بودی

که از قطره‌های برفِ کوهستانها جریان یافتی ،

از جلگه ها

و دشتها گذشتی

از زباله های روز مره و پلشتها گذشتی ،

از "ولگا" رستی و ،

به "گنگ" پیوستی

چه شد که اندرین باتلاقِ چرخه ی تولید و مصرف ،

دفع و بازیافت نشستی ؟!

دیگر اثری نمی بخشد

زلفِ سینه بر فشان و دست بر فرمان

خوش بران !

فاطی که باغ و بوستانش را وداع گفته ست

تا خدای اش را در بیابان های تفدیده بیابد ،

دستانش را ببین هماره به سوی آسمان

برای چند قطر ه ای باران

دراز است .

و ژیلا ، به تفکری سخت اندر نشسته ست

با نبضِ کوبانِ صبرش ،

 که رگهای اش را رشته ست ،

در انتظارِ دستی و دوستی ،

که بکارتِ ملتهبش را بنوازد .

آه ،

خموش ای پسرکِ ٤٠ ساله ی کوچولوی

"از قطره‌ها"

گوی چوگان در سرت ،

و آهنگِ سمِ ضربه ی سیاه اسبان

به صدایی که نمی آیدات به زبان .

×××

پوچی ی جاودان پیمای درونت ،

حریمِ هوایی مریخ را شکافته است ....

و خدا و شیطان ،

به پشتِ درهای بسته ،

برسرسرنوشت ات ،

چند قرنی پیش ،

به نیشخندی ،

به توافق رسیدند .

آه

این فروهرِ طلایی به دورِ گردنِ ات

ایرون که از بین نمیره ،

فقط خودتو بد جوری چزوندی

فکرِ دو روزِ دیگه ات کن ،

که سالات می آند سراغت ،

اون هم با چه عذابی ،

آخرِ عمری چجوری می خوای سر بزاری رو بالین و بخوابی

آذر ۸۸ – تهران

سبز هم که باشه

بتنهایی که صفایی نداره

رنگا تضاد می خوان و همخونی ،

تا تو رگ بره به نشیط خونی :

زردِ دوستی ،

بر سبزه ی زندگی ،

آبی عمیق بر نیلی ی سپید عاجی ،

خورشیدِ طلوع بر چمنِ شبنم آجین ،

ماه ی نافذِ عشق بر پنجه ی سرکشِ امواجی .

اگه سیا و سپید و رزد و به رنگِ ارغوون اس

انوار عشق بر همه اونها تابون اس

بخدا ،

داره دیر میشه ،

دلتم که داره هی پیر میشه ،

یهو به خودت می آی ،

می بینی همه فرصتارو سوزوندی ،

شاگردای گشنه ی مزدور

که پروا از خونی ندارن

چون می بینن ارباباشون

با زر و زورو ریا

رفتن نشسن اون بالا بالاها

به خود می گن راه اینه

منم می خوام ، سهم من کو ، یالا !

نکن برادر بخدا این خون توون داره سنگین

یه روزی سخت خشتکت رو می کشن پایین

بیآ برادر تو هم از همین آب و خاکی

تو چشمات نمی بینم هیچ نا پاکی

شیطونِ جهل رو تو مغزت پروار کردن

تا دس به سینه بیاستی هر وقت که صدا کردن

بیآ تا رنگهامون توی هم در آمیزیم

عجایب نقشی نادر تو این جهون طرح ریزیم

تک رنگی که معنایی نداره

اگه دردت نون و مقامه

کدوم بهتر به کامه :

تلاش و کار و سروری

یا کوبشِ چماقی بر سری ؟

دلم آتیش می گیره برات

که می دونم توی دلت داری یه حفره

که این نون می بری بر سر سفره

اما می دونم که بی گناه داری می سوزی

که از اربابت هست این آتیش افروزی

سر افرازی و بلند پروازی تو

دل اونو نمی کنه شاد

اون چماق داری می خواد ، گشنه ، بی سواد

تا به یه اشاره

تو خیابون بیآد

جیر بده بکنه پوره پاره

رهبرای فاسد که سیر مونی ندارن

زار بر خویشتن به سرود آیی :

تنم اسیر اهل و اعیاله

صبحم شب میشه در تامین نواله

ولی آخه این زندگی حقیر به پشیزی نمی ارزه

مگه آزادی که به چیزی نمی ارزه

این دو لقمه نون ِ لعنتی هم

به خدا به این همه هموطن ستیزی نمی ارزه

تو بخون منو با الله کبیرت آشنا کن

ولی کمی با خدای کوچک ِ دل ما هم صفا کن

از قرآن ِ مجیدت بخون سرود ِ حمد و سپاس

ولی شعرای ِ عاشقونه ما رو هم بشناس

بیآ در آغوشم بگیر

دردت رو بگو

تا عقلا مونو رو هم

بریزیم

راهی روشن کنیم جستجو

" زنجیر به خانه "

مسیرِ نوسانِ مدورِ مغزت

در خلاءیی نا ممکن

از دلانِ تنگِ نفرت گذشتن

به چمنِ سر سبزِ بار اندازی که به جان خریده ای ....

به گاهی که با چماقیِ زرین

فرقِ خواهرت را می شکافند

آیا عمرت دیگر به تکه نانی می ارزد ؟

نگاه یِ مدهوش ات

به زنجیرِ دورِ قلب ات

که درسرحدِ خاکِ خانه ات میخکوب شده است

در انتظارِ لحظه یِ انفجارِ آن تپشِ آهن دران

ضرب آهنگِ سرودِ یک بار زیستن یک بار مردن

تا بر زمینِ ناهموار نشینی و

با الفاظی که در کودکی آموخته ای

" بارش مغزها "

خش خش ِ اندیشه ای ترد
بر نازکای بسترات

پرواز ِ خیالی پروار
تا دور دست ِ محال

و پنجه ی لرزان ِ شبی
که گلوگاه ات را سخت فشرده ست
تا بارش ِ خاکستر ِ انفجار ِ مغز ات
بر سر سوگوارن ِ شهر نشیند

بهمن ۸۶

چونان روسپی ی خشکاندند !

تابستان ۸۸ زندان اوین

"میراث به عفونت نشسته"

بر خاکستر ِ گرم ِ خاک ،
بستر گزیدن

بوسه بر مخمل ِ آبی آسمان نهادن ،
بس تلخ است

از بیضه های به عفونت نشسته ی تاریخ افتادن
خموش و ابلهانه ،
به گذر ِ زمانه ی خویشتن نگریستن

غم ِ قرون ِ وسطا را گریستن
اندوه ی هزار و چهار صد سال ِ نکبت را زیستن

و انسانا !
حاصل ِ این منگ ِ روزگار ِ تنگ ِ پیچ ، چیست ؟! :

درمانده هرزه آیینی و ،
کهنه بغض ِ دیرینی
چکمه های چرمینی و ،
شلاق های خونینی
و کتابت ِ نفرینی ،
به زبانی بیگانه !

آه ای پدر ،
سرزمین ِ ما را ،

در چشمم .

تابستان ۱۳۸۸ زندان اوین

"مغلوب"

خشمم رقصان ،

بر پیچبادهای آزادی

××××

برای حق انسان ،

برای کودکی ،

نحیف و نو پای ،

که با من زاده شد .

برای اشکی ،

که در قلب من کاشته شد .

نگاشته به دست پدرانم ،

رشک نامه ای که قرنی پیش با شمشیرِ حماسه ای ،

در دلِ خاکِ وطن کاشته شد .

وکنون نگاهِ ی دریده ی گرسنه چشمان ،

بر پیکرِ برهنه ی مادرم .

و شرم جاری ،

انتظارا ،

نمی اشکی شبنم

بر وزش ِ آهی از جنس ِ خورشید ات ،

مهر روب غبارا

در مسیر ِ نخستین ِ نسیم ِ آزادی ِ سپیده دم

تابستان ۸۸ - زندان اوین

تهران

"نسیم آزادی"

وطن بر تن ،

مرا دیرین ،

از گذشتگانم غمی نفرین .

جنین وار ،

به خود تنیده اندر ،

فراسوی گذرگاه ی زمان

کله رُمبانِ تفکری وزین ،

در چهل قرون .

و قلبی

که چنون ،

از درون ،

کنون ،

خون می تپد

به عمق تاریخ ...

اینان دیگر از کدام ملت و تبارند ، به راستی از آنِ این دیارند !
کینچنین تخمِ نفرت در خاکت می کارند ، حرامی چنگیزند یا سکندرت ؟

درختانت سر بریدند ، دشتهای فرهنگسرایت به آتش کشیدند ،
می خانه‌ها ویران کردند، در آسیاب روان خونِ جوانان کردن ،
آن قومِ مدفوع خوار و تازی لشگرت !

ای وطن ! روزگارِ منگِ پیچِ ما را نگر ، اینان بر خلقِ خود می تازند !
سر مست هر شبی پاره ای از خاکت در قماری رسوا می بازند ،
وای ازین بختِ گزینِ اخترت !

تابستان -۸۸- تهران

"دوباره ایرانم آه"

دوباره ایرانم آه ، چرا خروشان چوسان ، ز همه اعضای پیکرت
زپای تا سرت ، فریادِ درد بر می کشی ، ز البرز تا خرم بندِ رت ؟

بس کن ! بی خودم کردی با این ضجه های جگر گداخته ات
اشک و عرق و خون را بفشان بر این زمینِ ناپارورت !

با این دلِ شکسته و دستِ بسته چگونه از نو بنایت کنم
پهن دشتِ سرِ سبزِ آزادِ آرزوهایم نهم در برابرت ؟

با این صدای بغض بگسسته چگونه بانگِ یاری طلب بلند سر دهم
با این تنِ به خون نشسته چون سر به راه نهم تا زکدامین سو آید سوار سرورت ؟

این زندگی حقیر به پشیزی نمی ارزد ، مگر آزادی به چیزی نمی ارزد
جان رنجورم ببین دیگر ز تیغِ دژخیمان نمی لرزد ، آن هم فدای افراشته سرت !

ز بینآلود تا سپید رود آمدم ، از سمرقند تا دِ ماوند آمدم ، از سیه جنگل
تا کوه ی کبود آمدم با تمام وجود آمدم تا سر نهم به نازنین برت !

هرگوشه پاره ای ز ترابِ بومت گویای حدِ یثِ کهن باره ای ، آزاد زیستن وبر
مرگ نگریستن ز کرد گردن کش آموزم و صبوری ز بلوچ زخمی در به درت !

آنکوراننده ای ز پیشت ، دستِ پلید کدامین فرزندِ بد عهدِ کج اندیشت
بر جای تاجِ رنگینت نهاده ست ، چنین جادوی الله اکبرت ؟

بودن آنها اطمینان داشته باشیم ، و داریم یاد میگیریم که آزادی با مکتبی که در ذات خود تبعیض می پروراند حاصل نمیشود و نیز نه از راه ی تفنگ ، و داریم یاد میگیریم.....شاید یکی از همین روزها یاد بگیریم !

امیدوارم در جایی اندر این گزیده به عقاید ِ درگونه ِ دیگران توهین نکرده باشم ...هر چند که گاه دلم بسیار ُ پر بود .

این شما و این هم "از راه و قطرهها"

من برای شنیدن ِ تمامی پیشنهادات و اعتقادات همواره آماده و بازم پس دوستان ...
نیش و نوش ِ خود را دریغ نفرمایند :

shahabshamloo@yahoo.com

آری عزیزان در این دور و زمانه سگ واقعا حق دارد صاحبش را گم کند !

هماره فکر کردم که آیا اصولا شعر در چنین شرایطی چه ارزشی یا بهتر بگویم چه اثری میتواند داشته باشد ؟! آیا توان ایجاد تغییر را دارد ؟ آیا میتواند انسانها را به بازگشت به ذات انسانی خود دعوت کند ؟
این را میدانم که اگر نوشته ای که ادعا دارد نوشته ای ست هنری به هر دلیلی از ایجاد تغییری ملموس و آنی در راه و روش انسانها عاجز باشد باید بتواند لااقل برای لحظاتی خواننده را از محیط خود خارج کرده ، اندیشه و احساس او را در جستجوی بر انگیخته تا در زمانی که به زمین برمیگردد حداقل ۱ سانتی به قد او و ارزشهای او افزوده شده باشد ، و دید او را گشوده و شهامت آزاد تر اندیشیدن ، آزادتر احساس کردن ، و آزاد تر سخن گفتن را به او عطا کند.
در غیر این صورت در حد ِ تنقلات ِ فکری تنزل پیدا میکند ، و یا شکلات ِ قلب ِ فربه مردان .

به هر حال تا اثری هنری به طور عام با دیگران در میان گذاشته نشود و مورد نقد قرار نگیرد نگارنده ی آن اثر نمی تواند پیشرفتی حاصل کند ....و ما تازه اول ِ راه ی آموختن ِ دموکراسی هستیم و داریم یاد میگیریم که دموکراسی ذهنیتی دموکراتیک می طلبد ...و داریم یاد میگیریم که تمامی حرفها را بشنویم و به تمامی باورهای دیگران احترام بگذاریم حتی اگر آنها را ناقص و ناکارآمد بدانیم ، و دل کسی را با نیش ِ خنجر ِ زبان خود ریش نکنیم ...نه به اشاره و نه به کنایه ...و اندیشه های خود را بر کسی تحمیل نکنیم هر چقدر به کامل و کارا

و دست بر سینه به اجداد خود قسم میخوریم که آنچه شنیده ایم عینِ
حقیقت است !
و اما دریغا ای دریغ !

و اما برگردم به مطلبِ اصلی که این داستان در چند صفحه پایان نمی
یابد و این رنجِ دانه را خاکی نیست .
و اما در گمگشته زمانه ای که بیشتر به مانندِ فسانه ای ست که در آن
جایزه ی صلحِ نوبل به کسی عطا میشود که توان لشگر کشی های عظیم
و آنچنانی را دارد و قرار داد های چند میلیاردی فروش تسلیحات راه
به راه منقد میکند تا دلارهای نفتی را به جیبِ خود باز گرداند و
حقوقِ کارگرانِ کار خانه های تسلیحاتی خود را با خون کسانی چون
من پرداخت نماید ، و در زمانه ای که خدا را با بهره های نجومی به
ارز یورو وام می دهند ، و در بیگانه زمانه ای که مرگ را هدیه پیچ
کرده و با پست ارسال می کنند ، و رهبرهای حیوان رُخسار از فلاکت
و فقرِ درماندگان بمب انتحاری یا به قول دوستان دری زبان بمب
خود کفانی می سازند ، و در زمانه ای بس غریبانه که در کشور عزیز ما
به نام خدا چها می کنند آنانی که خود را نماینده و بر گزیده خداوند
بر زمین می دانند و می خوانند و آنهم خدایی از جنسِ خودشان جبار
و خونریز و عقده ای که تحملِ کوچکترین انتقادی و یا حتی شکی را
ندارد !
آن یکی فکول کرواتی و اُتو کشیده که با یک اشارتِ انگشتش هزاران
هزار به خاک می غلتند و این یکی به مانندِ غارنشینانِ عصر حجر که به
شیوه ی سنتی با کنده و ساتور یکی یکی به نویت سر می برد ....و هر
دو دعوی طرفداری حقوقِ ترا دارند ...

پس شاید بهتر آن باشد که نام این کتاب را گزیده اشعار بنامیم و نه مجموعه .

و اما فکر میکنم که یک نویسنده یا شاعر اگر نه ۱۰۰۰ برابر حداقل ۱۰۰ برابر آنچه مینویسد باید بخواند و مطالعه کند ، که تا بستری منسجم فراهم گردد تا آب الهامش بر آن جریان یابد و کلامش از صلابت و کوبندگی برخوردار گردد....بخوان و بخوان و باز بخوان سپس خامه اندر نامه خوش بران !

و اما کاش انسانها هم نیز حداقل چند برابر آنچه فکر میکردند یا عمل میکردند مطالعه میکردند ...خاصه ما ایرانیها ...که دریغا اگر میکردیم از عواقب مخرب اسلام سیاسی آگاه میشدیم ، آنگاه که در اول پیدایش حکومت اسلامی در شهر مدینه چگونه آیات مهر و محبت و برادر دوستی که نخست در مکه نگا شته شده بود به محض به قدرت رسیدن لشگر اسلام به ضرب ِ شمشیر به پیام ِ خون و خونریزی و عدم تحمل باورهای دیگران مبدل گشت .

و خوب می فهمیدیم که تغییرو جهشی که از راه ی زور و اسلحه حاصل میشود باید از همان راه ی خشونت دوام یابد .

و اما نمی دانم که درد ِ خود پسندی ست یا تنبلی که ما ها دوست داریم دیگران به جای مازحمت ِ مطالعه را کشیده و چکیده دریافتهای خود را به ما ارایه دهند .

هم از این روست که هرآنچه اهداف آنها را تامین میکند به مغز ما تزریق میکنند !

و ما چون مونگولها با چهرهایی مات و لبهایی باد کرده خاموش نگریسته و در تا یید آنها سر میجنبا نیم !

به یکباره بی کوچکترین تاملی در غیاب شاعر نگاشته میشود : در فراسوهای دور آنجا که آهوان بی گناهی با تنی زخمی از درندگان دشت ِ بی صفت پناه می جویند تا از چشمه های پاکی آب بنوشند ، یا در اعماق ِ تیره ی جنگلی کشف ناشده با میوههای ناب و نایاب که کسی هنوز با طعم آنها آشنا نیست ، یا در آتش گندمزاری خشک که شعله های آن به سوی آسمانها در اعتراض زبانه می کشد ، و یا بر پنجه ی سرکش ِ امواج ِ دریایی دور و گمشده که بر ورای ساحل ِ تخیل بشری می کوبد ...و ....یا ....و... . چنین کارهایی در جا در روح و جان انسان حک میشود و تا آخر عمر در ذهن آدمی باقی می ماند . به مانند ِ کارهایی که در انفرادی های اوین در قلب دریده ام جاری گشت و بی هیچ کاغذ و قلمی با خون در دلم نوشته شد تا دایم بر لب آنها را زمزمه کنم تا مونس شبهای بی روزنم باشند .

هر چند که باید اعتراف کنم در برخی ازاین کارها تنها چند بیتی نخست ناخودآگاه جاری گشته و سپس با اندیشه تکمیل شده است و اما بسیاری از آنها به طور کامل به یکبارگی شکل گرفته است و بی هیچ سا خته ای وپرداخته ای در این کتاب عرضه شده است .
این به خوبی در شبه غزلها قابل مشاهده است تا آنجایی که کار را جهت قافیه بندی اصلاح نکردم و گذاشتم تا همانطور به صورت خام یا بهتر بگویم همانگونه که جاری شده است ارایه گردد . هم از این روست که دست به حذف ِ بسیاری از کارهای خود زدم ...تا بیشترنوشته های چاپ شده از این گونه خاص و نادر باشند ، تا اگر نه به طور کامل تا حد ِ زیادی از این کار راضی باشم .

به نام انسان

با درود ،

در این زمانه ی در به در که انسان از انعکاس ِ خود هراسان و از خانه
ی خود گریزان است ، و در شهری رنگارنگ و پرتپش که بر سر حد ِ
دو قاره خفته است که در آن چهرهای سرد به مانند ِ اسکناسی متحرک
به آدمی می نگرند ....گفتم حال که دیگر سودای بازگشت به وطن در
سر نیست مجموعه ی نوشته های ام را جهت ِ چاپ گرد آوری کنم . و
چون زمان فراوان داشتم ، تا آقای قاچاقچی محترم که بر حسب ِ
خوش اقبالی هم زبانی ست با لهجه ی نُقلی دری ما را به مقصد ِ یکی
از کشورهای اروپای شمالی بارنامه کند ، انجایی که گویند آزادی ِ
آدمی را ارج می نهند و حقوقش را بی خدشه ای درج کردند ، ترجمه
ی کارهای ام را نیزشعرگونه فراهم کردم . و چون به لطف ِ بزرگ ِ
شدن در خانه ای دو زبانه از دیر باز آموخته ام که به دو زبان
بیاندیشم ، تا بر حسب ِ الهام فرود آمده الفاظ گاه به پارسی و گاه به
انگلیسی از قلمم جاری شود ، ترجمه ها بدکی از آب در نیآمده ست و
شخصا تا حد ِ ۶۰-۵۰ درصدی ار آنها راضی هستم. در ضمن اشعاری
اندر این کتاب موجود است که در اصل به زبان انگلیسی سروده شده
است ، که دیگر دلیلی ندیدم آنها را به فارسی برگردانم و به ترجمه ی
کارها از فارسی به انگلیسی بسنده کردم ، به استثنای یک شعر به نام "از
راه " که احساس کردم ترجمه ی این کار به فارسی میتواند اندکی به
بار این کتاب بیافزاید .
این را نیز بگویم که به نظر شخصی من تمامی آثارم از ارزش ِ هنری
بارزی برخوردار نیستند و فقط کارهای را می پسندم و قبول دارم که

شریک شیطان
نسیم شبانه

از راه و قطرهها

شهاب شاملو (خموش)